Teri –

Rest in the comfort
of God's boundless love

Carol

# Ripples of God's Love

## POEMS TO REFRESH THE SOUL

### CAROL CROUCH

iUniverse, Inc.
Bloomington

# Ripples of God's Love
## Poems to Refresh the Soul

*iUniverse books may be ordered through booksellers or by contacting:*

*iUniverse*
*1663 Liberty Drive*
*Bloomington, IN 47403*
*www.iuniverse.com*
*1-800-Authors (1-800-288-4677)*

*Because of the dynamic nature of the Internet, any Web addresses or links contained in this book may have changed since publication and may no longer be valid. The views expressed in this work are solely those of the author and do not necessarily reflect the views of the publisher, and the publisher hereby disclaims any responsibility for them.*

*Any people depicted in stock imagery provided by Thinkstock are models, and such images are being used for illustrative purposes only.*

Unless otherwise noted, scripture quotations are taken from the New Living Translation, *NLT Study Bible*, 2nd ed. (Carol Stream, IL: Tyndale House Publishers, 2008).

Scriptures noted "NIV," "Amp," or "KJV" are taken from *The Comparative Study Bible*, rev. ed. (Grand Rapids, MI: Zondervan, 1999).

Scriptures noted "NKJV" are taken from *The Essential Evangelical Parallel Bible* (New York: Oxford University Press, 2004).

*Certain stock imagery © Thinkstock.*

*ISBN: 978-1-4502-8188-1 (pbk)*
*ISBN: 978-1-4502-8187-4 (cloth)*
*ISBN: 978-1-4502-8186-7 (ebk)*

*Library of Congress Control Number: 2010919365*

*Printed in the United States of America*

*iUniverse rev. date: 1/13/11*

To Norman, my husband and partner of many years, who supported and encouraged me  in this work of love throughout its creation;

To David, Michael, and Laura, our three children; and to their spouses, Kay, Tracy, and Nathan; and to all our wonderful grandchildren, who provided by their living witness many experiences that give color to the words I have written;

And to many friends and members of our extended family who encouraged me to bring these poems to a wider audience:

You are loved, appreciated, and valued for the role each of you played as the work progressed.

No power … indeed, nothing in all creation will
ever be able to separate us from the love of God
that is revealed in Christ Jesus our Lord.
Romans 8:39

# Preface

"The faithful love of the Lord never ends! His mercies never cease. Great is his faithfulness; his mercies begin afresh each morning ... The Lord is good to those who depend on him, to those who search for him" (Lamentations 3:22–23, 25). These words underlie my faith. They are universal in their extent. They embrace every emotion and need we may have; they emphasize the changeless love of God, his reliability, and his presence that never leaves our sides. The love and faithfulness of God and the indwelling presence of the Holy Spirit of God are the birthright of every person who believes in Jesus Christ.

For many years, as far back as my teenage years, I have journaled my responses to the ambiguities of life, to its good and difficult times, and to the effects of changing circumstances. These responses are not unique to me. Usually, the words begin to form in my mind as I consider feelings or thoughts. When fully written out, they are a reflection of my faith in God and the need to remain focused on him. They affirm the faithfulness of God in my life—his closeness, help, comfort, and love.

My love of the beauty and complexity of nature is woven into the words. Growing up on a small farm in Wisconsin, I was fascinated by the enormous diversity of the natural world. As I grew, these observations and the interrelationships I saw became the basis for an appreciation and awe of God's creation.

I have experienced many years of chronic pain and the fluctuating feelings and emotions that accompany it. Always, God in his love and compassion has embraced me. I believe that my faith is deeper, more relevant, and more intimately related to Jesus Christ through the countless times I have called out, "Help me!"

Through poetry written in response to prayer, I hope to share perspective and insights that I believe have been conveyed to my mind and spirit. My prayer is that each of these writings will speak to the spirit of someone. In Christ, we have the privilege of living with joy whether our world is crashing in around us, or the path ahead is straight with no diversions. Joy in worship and prayer and knowing the love of God and his acceptance of us as we are also are of vital importance in living out our faith.

Jesus died and was raised victorious over death and sin, giving us freedom, everlasting life, hope, courage, and the assurance that he is always present in our lives even when we feel alone, overwhelmed, and perhaps forgotten. The presence of Jesus seems almost palpable to me in times of difficulty, but also in times of joy. He provides the strength to endure with hope; his love embraces me then as well as in times of joy.

May all who read these words find comfort in the faithful presence of Jesus Christ. May your life never be the same as you allow his love to embrace you. May ripples of God's love move ever outward from your service in his name.

In his everlasting love,

Carol Crouch

# Contents

# PROLOGUE

# A King Is Born

For a child is born to us, a son is given to us. The government
will rest on his shoulders, and he will be called: Wonderful
Counselor, Mighty God, Everlasting Father, Prince of
Peace. His government and its peace will never end.
Isaiah 9:6–7

He came into the very world he created, but the world didn't
recognize him. He came to his own people, and even they rejected
him. But to all who believed him and accepted him, he gave the right
to become children of God ... So the Word became human and made
his home among us. He was full of unfailing love and faithfulness.
John 1:10–12, 14

The incredible greatness of God's power for us who believe in him
... is the same mighty power that raised Christ from the dead and
seated him in the place of honor at God's right hand in the heavenly
realms. Now he is far above any ruler or authority or power or
leader or anything else—not only in this world but also in the world
to come. God has put all things under the authority of Christ and
has made him head over all things for the benefit of the church.
Ephesians 1:19–22

~ ~ ~ ~ ~

A child was born long ago,
Sent to be the king of nations.
His birth took place in a humble shed;
The breath of livestock warmed the air.

His mother wrapped him in soft woven cloth,
Held him close, overwhelmed with awe.
The holy child, sent from heaven,
Nestled in her loving arms.

Ancient scriptures foretold his birth
To an unknown girl in a captive nation.
Her hopes and dreams were limited
By her quiet life in a tiny village.

Her people longed for a conquering leader,
A king to wield majestic power.
Her child grew unnoticed by men,
Absorbing prophecy pointing to him.

His family came from a royal line
Of kings descended from a shepherd.
They lived among a chosen people,
Waiting for their savior-king.

One sunny day, he strode away
To teach and heal and call disciples.
He taught of a kingdom established in heaven,
A kingdom founded on truth and love.

Born of the Spirit, secured in hearts,
It welcomed those who believed in him.
But the words of Jesus caused alarm
To leaders bound by ancient tradition.

Three years later, the religious leaders,
Tiring of Jesus's righteous condemnation,
Joined the enemy to put to death
The Son of Man with his disturbing words.

They conspired to arrest him secretly
When those who welcomed his message of love
Could not interfere with their careful plans;
They were helping fulfill God's plan for the nations.

His mother anguished near the cross
On which his tortured body hung.
She recalled a prophecy spoken to her
Of a sword that would pierce her tender heart.

The authorities thought they were done with him;
Their actions merely fulfilled the prophecies.
As his father in heaven raised him to life,
A power was released that conquered death.

The risen Lord rejoined his disciples,
Reassured them that his reign is eternal.
The news spread like wildfire;
Nothing could halt its powerful message.

Spiritual darkness held humanity in its grip;
Now the human spirit was freed.
It soared beyond imposed restraint;
Joy and peace filled those who believed.

Two millennia later, though still embattled,
That message gives wings to the human spirit.
Trials and pain are placed in perspective
By the presence and care of the God who loves.

The Spirit of Jesus is active on earth
Bringing spiritual freedom to all who believe.
The grace of God is the key to the kingdom;
Our life decisions turn the key.

The kingdom of heaven here on earth
Lives in the hearts of imperfect believers
Who triumph over the darkness they find,
Leaving a model for others to follow.

Their hope is based in the heavenly kingdom
Where Jesus Christ reigns unopposed.
The things of Earth lose importance
When things of God come first in their hearts.

# PRAISE and WORSHIP

# Worship in Spirit and Truth

God is Spirit, so those who worship him
must worship in spirit and in truth.
John 4:24

Come, let us sing to the Lord!
Let us shout to the Rock of our salvation.
Let us come with thanksgiving,
Let us sing psalms of praise to him.
For the Lord is a great God,
A great King above all gods ...
Come, let us worship and bow down.
Let us kneel before the Lord our maker, for he is our God.
Psalm 95:1–3, 6

Everyone has sinned; we all fall short of God's glorious standard.
Yet God, with undeserved kindness, declares that we are
righteous ... through Christ Jesus. For God presented Jesus
as the sacrifice for sin. People are made right with God when
they believe that Jesus sacrificed his life, shedding his blood.
Romans 3:23–25

In him we live and move and exist. As some of your
own poets have said, "We are his children."
Acts 17:28

~ ~ ~ ~ ~

Worship is intended to express joy, honor, devotion, adoration, and love
to our sovereign God as we acknowledge his greatness and his presence
among us. However, sometimes, our hearts are not in the words we
say. There is little spontaneity or rejoicing. We are not able to allow the
words to speak to us and lighten our spirits. But worship is declaring
an attitude of praise: "God is in his heaven and in control of this world

that seems to be going many directions at once. Lay your burden at his feet and relish him."

In Psalm 34:4–5, 8, the psalmist says, "I prayed to the Lord and he answered me. He freed me from all my fears. Those who look to him for help will be radiant with joy … Taste and see that the Lord is good."

We are like the old time farmer who may have never traveled more than a few miles from his birthplace. Spiritually, we seldom venture beyond our current comfort zones in worship. We put God in a box. We wear blinders to prevent distraction like a horse pulling a plow. We keep our attention on the furrow and plow the soil without passion, not diverting from our familiar routines.

The Psalms name instruments to be used in worship. Those Psalms devoted to praise and worship are vibrant in expression. The Israelites were a thankful people in response to the gracious actions of their God. He had chosen them because he loved them, not because of what they did or who they were. Typically, their worship expressed their awe of God and their thankfulness. During the period of the kings of Israel and later, those of Judah, their worship was in an atmosphere of rejoicing with music, shouting, and dancing. But it was also characterized by such things as prayers, vows, and sacred meals.[1]

The Jewish people and the early Christian church knew what their savior, God, had brought about to preserve their lives. For Christians, this was even more significant because they believed that Jesus Christ, the Son of God, freely gave his own life to bring salvation, the forgiveness of sin, to each who believed.

No groups of people before had ever seen such mighty saving acts on their behalf, such love expressed by the living God. The God of the Old Testament was too holy and sublime, too transcendent, too all powerful to allow an image carved of wood or rock to represent him. The God of the New Testament sent his own Son to live as one of us on earth, to die the death of a criminal, and by his mighty power, to raise him from the dead in the Resurrection. By his action, all people could have a living, breathing, personal relationship with him.[2] This same mighty power is available through the Holy Spirit to all who believe in him.[3]

By his sacrificial death, Jesus Christ removed the barrier that separates us from God, the presence of sin in our lives, by providing forgiveness of sin through the cross.

Our lifestyle is far removed from that of those early keepers of the faith. Nevertheless, we can give our full attention to God, and worship him from the depth of our hearts. The form of our expressions of love, adoration, and gratitude will vary widely. But God is asking for *all* of us when we worship—our committed love, trust, joy, attention, and participation in response to his gift of new life in Christ. When we worship in spirit and truth, we, too, will sense his Spirit in our midst.

# A Song of Love

I led Israel along with my ropes of kindness and love.
Hosea 11:4

It is good to give thanks to the Lord, to sing praises to the Most High.
Psalm 92:1

He has removed our sins from us as far as the east is from the west.
Psalm 103:12

~~~~~

I sing praises to you, O Lord,
For your kindness and love to me.
Before my birth, you knew me
And planned good things for me.

Your gentle voice, it wooed me;
With cords of love, you drew me.
Your patience never wavered
While my sight was blinded to you.

A hollow sense of emptiness
Filled my every action.
A worldly life of pleasure
Lost its allure and thrill.

I longed for things of value—
Enthusiasm, relationship, love.
Your heart reached out to mine
Through one who lived for you.

I sensed the joy of your presence;
My heart leaped high with hope.
My quest for acceptance was over;
You received me though burdened with sin.

The past is a slate wiped clean;
The future glows with promise.
Today is all I have
To serve that others may see.

# The Majesty of Creation in Christ

O Lord, what a variety of things you have made! In wisdom you
have made them all. The earth is full of your creatures. Here is
the ocean, vast and wide, teeming with life of every kind, both
large and small ... The Lord takes pleasure in all he has made!
Psalm 104: 24–25, 31

[Jesus] is the God who created the world and everything in it.
Acts 17:24

In the beginning the Word already existed. The Word was with God,
and the Word was God ... God created everything through him.
John 1:1, 3

~ ~ ~ ~

Eagles soar on currents of air;
A butterfly sips nectar with uncurled tongue.
A dragonfly darts, just beyond reach;
    Rays of color glance from its wings.

Giant whales frolic in the waves;
Sea lions bark on a massive rock.
A seagull dives from impressive height
    To grab a fish only it can see.

Waves crash in with resounding thunder,
Carving the rocks that guard the shore.
Winds blowing free across the beach
    Shape a tree into twisted form.

In the freshness of earth after a shower,
A brilliant rainbow floats in the sky.
Raindrops tremble tenuously
    Like miniature jewels reflecting light.

The mystery of a newborn child,
Perfect in design, innocent for an instant,
Till its first cry when it perceives
Its mother is there to meet its needs.

Jesus came as a tiny babe—
Son of God and Son of Man.
Perfection in spirit and as one of us;
The Word of God created all we see.

# Blessing upon Blessing

From his abundance we have all received one
gracious blessing after another.
John 1:16

Thank you for making me so wonderfully complex!
Your workmanship is marvelous.
Psalm 139:14

~~~~~

Salvation, love, strength, and peace,
Family, friends, and daily bread—
All are gifts from our Father in heaven.

Eyes to see creation's glory
In stately forest, majestic mountain,
In delicate flower and butterfly.

Ears to hear wind whisper through trees,
Songs of birds perched high on a branch,
Soaring music inspired by God.

Smell to sense a flower's fragrance;
Earthy scent after a shower
Settles the dust of a hot, dry day.

Touch to feel another's embrace,
A child's trusting, tiny hand,
The softness of a baby's skin.

Air to breathe moment by moment,
The gift of life to give God glory;
Freedom of spirit through Christ, his son.

A marvelous mind to search for purpose;
Our spirit returns God's gracious love;
Creation proclaims the perfection of God.

The spirit that he gave to us
Reflects his Spirit who dwells within,
Forming a unity only we may enjoy.

We are special in his sight—
Each one counts around the world.
Rejoicing, we praise our Savior and Lord.

# Hymn of Praise

Sing songs and hymns and spiritual songs
to God with thankful hearts.
Colossians 3:16

Everything on earth will worship you; they will sing your
praises, shouting your name in glorious songs.
Psalm 66:4

~~~~~

Almighty Father, my Lord and King,
I see your hand in everything:
In a golden sunset tinged with red,
In caring words that someone said,
In the far-flung stars that dot the sky,
In a towering tree that reaches so high.

Graceful ferns near a tumbling brook,
Browsing deer in a shadowed nook,
A shiny green beetle scurrying by,
The song of a bird in clear blue sky,
Majestic mountains crowned with white,
Meadow flowers, with blossoms bright.

You planned this great diversity,
Gave ears to hear and eyes to see.
Oh, may I never grow deaf or blind
To the myriad wonders that here I find.
I will never tire of giving praise
To the one who gladdens all my days.

# UNIQUE in CHRIST

# The Rosebud

The Lord will guide you continually, giving you
water when you are dry and restoring your strength.
You will be like a well-watered garden.
Isaiah 58:11

I am the vine; you are the branches. Those who remain[4]
in me, and I in them, will produce much fruit.
John 15:5

~~~~~

I am like a rosebud,
Petals tightly furled.
The sunshine of God's love
Provides it light to grow;
Life-giving nourishment
Flows up through its stem.

Its petals open wide,
Exposing fragile beauty.
Fragrance fills the air,
Floating on the breeze.
Butterflies flitting by
Are attracted by its fragrance.

As I abide in Christ,
His Spirit flows through me.
He gives light and love;
I respond with lasting fruit—
Fruit of love and joy,
A fragrant offering to God.

His garden is worldwide,
Filled with color bright.
Everyone is special,
Treasured as he is.
Together, they bring glory
To the God who gave them life.

# Weeds and Jewels

The stone that the builders rejected has now become the
cornerstone. This is the Lord's doing, and it is wonderful to see.
Mark 12:10–11

How precious are your thoughts about me,
O God. They cannot be numbered.
Psalm 139:17

~ ~ ~ ~ ~

They were only weeds,
  dried up, fragile, and brown,
    their seeds tossed and scattered
      by the breezes blowing by.
Unwanted, they dried up,
  ignored and disdained;
    no one glanced at them.
But potential beauty lay hidden,
  unseen by human eye.

An artist passing by
  saw beauty in their form;
    he gathered and transformed them
      by covering them with gold.
By his gracious touch,
  thistles sparkled bright;
    burdock was bejeweled,
      Queen Anne's lace was stars.

Like faded, rejected weeds,
      we sometimes feel unnoticed,
      unneeded, and unwanted.
But Jesus chooses us,
      sees potential deep within,
      satisfies our yearning
          to live a richer life.
He transforms, renews our lives,
      makes us a new creation.
He prepares us for his kingdom,
      unites us all in him.

# Snowflakes

He knows how weak we are; he remembers we are only dust.
Psalm 103:14

When the right time came, God sent his Son born of
a woman … And because we are his children, God
has sent the Spirit of his Son into our hearts.
Galatians 4:4

A lamp is placed on a stand where it gives light to everyone in
the house. In the same way, let your good deeds shine out for
all to see, so that everyone will praise your heavenly Father.
Matthew 5:15–16

Live clean, innocent lives as children of God, shining like
bright lights in a world full of crooked and perverse people.
Philippians 2:15

~ ~ ~ ~ ~

Snowflakes form 'round specks of dust,
Each one different from all the rest.
Floating down, they cover the earth,
Transforming, renewing, wherever they fall.

On a starlit night, God sent his Son,
The Savior of men to be born like us.
He brought God's grace and light and truth;
To all who believed, he offered life.

He showed us that we are unique,
Called to fill a special nook.
No one else can fill the places
That God prepared before our births.

Renewed in Christ, we are commissioned
To share the truth he came to bear
Far and wide, over all the earth,
Till each has heard about God's love.

As snowflakes change the place they fall,
We make a difference where we are.
Snow crystals sparkle, reflecting the light;
The good we do shines like a lamp.

# Worth in Christ

God saved us and called us to live a holy life. He did this, not
because we deserved it, but because that was his plan from before
the beginning of time—to show us his grace through Jesus Christ.
II Timothy 1:9

God shows no favoritism. In every nation he accepts
those who fear him and do what is right.
Acts 10:34–35

The King [Jesus Christ] will say to [those who have served him] …
"I was hungry, and you fed me. I was thirsty, and you gave a drink.
I was a stranger, and you invited me into your home. I was naked,
and you gave me clothing. I was sick, and you cared for me. I was
in prison and you visited me … When you did it to one of the
least of these my brothers and sisters, you were doing it to me."
Matthew 25:34–36, 40

~ ~ ~ ~ ~

What are we worth to God? The scriptures clearly declare that we were
worth the sacrificial death of Jesus to restore us to a vital, mutual love
relationship with him. We may question our importance, or worth, to
God. But the answer never changes; we are of infinite worth.

Jesus knows us in a way that is difficult to comprehend. All our feelings
and thoughts are known more deeply than we can imagine, but through
a screen of grace. He knew us before we were born—"all the days
ordained for me were written in your book before one of them came
to be." [5] That is, he foreknew both our trials and our joys, and he has
promised, "I will not fail you or abandon you."[6]

Because he loved the world, by his grace and mercy, God sent Jesus,
his Son, to redeem us from our sin. He spent the last night before his
arrest in the peaceful Garden of Gethsemane among ancient olive
trees. In agony of spirit, he prayed to be spared this cup, this way of

reconciling the separation between God and humanity. An angel from heaven appeared and strengthened him. His sweat fell profusely to the ground.[7] But his thoughts and prayers that night were centered on the will and purpose of his father. His attention to his destiny could not be distracted, even though he understood, far more than we can perceive in our sheltered lives, all that it would cost his earthly body to suffer a brutal death on a rough-hewn cross made of beams of wood.

His emotions and senses screamed silently in the anguish of unimaginable pain, loneliness, and fatigue borne not only as Son of Man, but even more as Son of God. During the long hours before his death, struggling for every breath, he suffered physical thirst and agony of body and mind. Feeling abandoned even by God, bearing the sins of humanity, he cried out to him in the darkest moment of his life: "My God, my God, why have you abandoned me?"[8]

It is beyond human comprehension to understand the loneliness Jesus suffered at this point in his ordeal. God could not be identified with him as he bore the sins of the world. For the only time in eternity, he was alone. "Then Jesus uttered another loud cry and breathed his last. And the curtain in the sanctuary of the Temple was torn in two, from top to bottom."[9]

His body was laid in a cold, dark tomb of stone. But three days later, in the misty dawn of a new day, the mighty power of God restored his life—the same power to which we each have access.[10] In the momentous event of the Resurrection, he reigned victorious over the powers of sin and death.

Several weeks later, following a period of united prayer among a group of those closest to Jesus, the Holy Spirit indwelt believers for the first time. They exploded with joy, commitment, and action. The Gospel message—good news for every nation—flew out from Jerusalem as quickly as God-appointed messengers were able to travel. It could not be stopped. God was in control, and his message was both life changing and life giving.

As the Gospel spread, it carried with it a widened concept of the individual worth of men and women, children, and slaves and free people of all races. Over the centuries, it permeated society. Jesus not only gives us vibrant new life in him; he also teaches a new sense of the worth of every living person. No matter how feeble, handicapped, young, or old; no matter the circumstances that shape one's environment, in the hopelessness of a slum or grandeur of a mansion; whether one serves, or is among those who are neediest; each is of value in some sense. Each one can have an influence, whether he or she lives a day or a century. Each has an innate, God-given spark that fuels his or her life.

We have been given a mandate to serve[11] those who would otherwise have little hope and to restore within them a sense of value for their individual lives.

# THE GRACIOUS LOVE

of

GOD

# The Greatest Gift

In the beginning the Word already existed. The
Word was with God, and the Word was God.
John 1:1

God saved you by his grace when you believed. And
you can't take credit for this; it is a gift from God.
Ephesians 2:8

Christ has truly set us free [from the bondage of sin].
Galations 5:1

~~~~~

I used to try to face each day
On my own strength, in my own way.
Within my soul, there was unrest
And I set out on a long, long quest
To find the peace for which I yearned;
In the end, it was to God I turned.

His love had always followed me,
But I had been unable to see
Through mists of darkness before my face.
Now was revealed his infinite grace.
To redeem us all, God sent his Son;
By faith in him, salvation I won.

He freed me from the bondage of sin,
Gave me joy and peace within.
Let Jesus, my Savior, be your Savior, too.
Serve him joyfully; to him be true.
Allowing him to direct your way
Provides a lamp day by day.

Don't wait too long; to him draw near;
His perfect love will conquer fear.
Your actions will reflect his mind
As he shapes you and refines.
Answer now his gracious call—
Receive the greatest gift of all.

New life by grace is freely offered,
A gift to those who trust his word.
Acclaim him then as Lord and King
And join with me as together we sing
Hosannas of praise to his wonderful name;
He remains forever and ever the same.

# Joseph's Robe

Jacob loved Joseph more than any of his other children ... So one day Jacob had a special gift made for Joseph—a beautiful robe. But his brothers hated Joseph because their father loved him more than the rest of them ... [Much later, Joseph said to his brothers,] "God has sent me here ahead of you to keep you and your families alive and to preserve many survivors. So it was God who sent me here, not you! And he is the one who made me an advisor to Pharaoh."
Genesis 37:3–4; 45:7–8

Anyone who belongs to Christ has become a new person.
The old life has gone; a new life has begun.
II Corinthians 5:17

~ ~ ~ ~ ~

Jacob, a doting father, presented his favorite son with a costly robe, beautifully designed. It represented favor, privilege, and a close relationship with his father. However, Joseph was an immature and boastful young man who soon found himself at odds with his brothers, who were shepherds tending their father's flocks of sheep.

Joseph's favored standing and resultant self-righteousness led to his brothers' jealous conspiracy to sell him into Egypt as a slave and fake his death. Many years later, when Joseph had risen to favor in Egypt, he became a means of salvation for his family from a widespread famine in that region. Ultimately, this humanistic salvation, although within the providence of God, grew into spiritual salvation[12] for all the families of the world through the saving work of Jesus Christ.

"In Christ, there is no favoritism."[13] The love of God cannot by his nature be less or more. God *is* love. If we believe and accept Jesus Christ, he gives us the right to become children of God,[14] and God welcomes us into his family.

Our relationship with Christ is as close as we allow, or enable, it to be. Jesus will not force himself into our lives. But when we look wholeheartedly for him, we will find him.[15] If he seems absent, it may be we who left. This does not discount the "famine" times many faithful Christians sometimes experience when it may seem their prayers are going nowhere. However, even these can be times of growth.

A close relationship requires our genuine input. Salvation, the gift of life through Christ, is a beautiful "robe" that covers our sins. It is a precious gift available only through the sacrificial death of Jesus. But it must be opened, and accepted, before we receive its benefit of new life in Christ. Building a fulfilling relationship requires regular tending, conversation in prayer, knowledge of the word of God, growth in Jesus Christ, and fellowship with other believers.

There is no need to win the love of God. He loved us before we were born. It can only be accepted as we live our lives within his will to the best of our human ability.

# The Shepherd and His Lamb

If a man has a hundred sheep and one of them gets lost,
[he will] leave the ninety-nine others in the wilderness
and search for the one that is lost ... When he has found
it, he will joyfully carry it home on his shoulders.
Luke 15:4–5

He will feed his flock like a shepherd. He will carry the
lambs in his arms, holding them close to his heart.
Isaiah 40:11

~ ~ ~ ~ ~

As the shepherd counted his sheep that night,
The count fell short; one lamb was gone.
He closed the gate that kept them safe,
Took up his staff and left alone.

He strode with purpose toward the pasture,
Searching and calling as he went along.
How he rejoiced, when he found that lamb—
He carried it home, in his heart a song.

When safely back, he removed the burrs
That caught on its wool while it was astray.
He soothed abrasions it had suffered,
Rubbed its back in a tender way.

Like a shepherd, Jesus came.
He loves each lamb, and when we stray,
He mourns the absence of even one;
He woos us gently from our wanton ways.

For only by following him each day
Can we be truly in tune with his plan.
It is only then that we understand
The magnitude of his love for man.

# FAITH

# Faith Is Like a Plant

Let us run with endurance the race God has set before
us. We do this by keeping our eyes on Jesus, the
champion who initiates and perfects our faith.
Hebrews 12:1–2

I pray that from his glorious, unlimited resources he will
empower you with inner strength through his Spirit Then Christ
will make his home in your hearts as you trust in him. Your
roots will grow down into God's love and keep you strong.
Ephesians 3:16–17

Your faith is flourishing and your love for one another is growing.
We proudly tell God's other churches about your endurance
and faithfulness in … the hardships you are suffering.
II Thessalonians 1:2–3

~ ~ ~ ~ ~

Faith is like a plant.

A tiny leaf grows skyward,
    seeking water and light.
Slowly, with commitment,
    it reaches for the sun;
    its nature is to grow.
With inborn drive and persistence;
    it survives the storms of life,
    building inner strength.

In the united body of Christ,
    faith finds fertile soil
    and a beckoning light.
We strengthen one another;
    rooted deep in Christ,

our faith in him increases.
As we grope and search for meaning,
we grow in loving response
to Jesus's assuring presence.

The resilient strength of faith
reflects Christ's power within;
The inner presence of Christ
reveals his love to all.
His church grows by love
and unity in the Spirit,
And the unified body of Christ
will be forever strong.

# Destination by Faith

God blesses those who patiently endure testing and
temptation. Afterward they will receive the crown of life
that God has promised to those who love him.
James 1:12

The gateway to life is very narrow and the road
is difficult, and only a few ever find it.
Matthew 7:14

If any of you wants to be my follower, you must turn from
your selfish ways, take up your cross and follow me.[16]
Mark 8:34

Your own ears will hear him. Right behind you a voice will say,
"This is the way you should go," whether to the right or to the left.
Isaiah 30:21

~~~~~

When Jesus invited, "Follow me,"
He taught that we must abandon self.
We must depend on him alone,
Trusting him to get us home.

Slowly, surely, we make our way
On a narrow path, by day and night.
His presence never leaves our side;
He cares for us while we sleep.

Dangers and difficulties cross the path;
He carries us when the way is hard.
When on safer ground we walk,
He is there to refresh our spirits.

Our strength increases as we learn his way.
Though we may straggle at difficult times,
Our faith weak kneed, and out of breath,
He faithfully encourages, "Do your best."

Then we receive a second wind;
Our faith restored, our trust renewed,
We know beyond any doubt
Jesus leads us to eternal bliss.

# Stairway of Faith

Jacob found a stone to rest his head against and lay down to sleep. As he slept, he dreamed of a stairway that reached from the earth up to heaven. And he saw the angels of God going up and down the stairway. At the top of the stairway stood the Lord.
Genesis 28:12

The Son of Man is the stairway between heaven and earth.
John 1:51

Restore to me the joy of your salvation, and make me willing to obey you ... The sacrifice you desire is a broken spirit. You will not reject a broken and repentant heart, O God.
Psalm 51:12, 17

Your faith is growing more and more, and the love every one of you has for each other is increasing.
II Thessalonians 1:2 (NIV)

~ ~ ~ ~ ~

Faith is acquired step by step.
Year by year, it grows more sure
As obedience to the will of God
Narrows the choices made each day.

Dependence on self is left behind
As trust in Jesus takes its place.
When he is allowed to hold the reins,
We enjoy a life made whole like his.

Trials may come as we progress,
But Jesus provides grace and strength.
Our endurance grows ever stronger;
Storms bring out the grit in us.

Character emerges as we persist,
Giving confidence in our new lives.
No step on the stairs can be skipped;
Each has lessons for life in Christ.

Rewards accrue with each new step—
Peace that passes understanding,
Joy of life through good and bad,
Knowing Jesus's changeless love.

When we have reached the highest step,
The Lord warmly welcomes us
With, "Well done, good and faithful servant";
We know that we have won our rest.

Jesus is the only bridge
From life on earth to life eternal.
By trusting in his grace and mercy,
We walk across his bridge of love.

We enter into his holy kingdom;
We sing with joy and praise his name.
Our work on earth has been well done;
Life with him is our reward.

# Faith Perfected

Let us strip off every weight that slows us down, especially the sin that so easily trips us up. And let us run with endurance the race God has set before us. We do this by keeping our eyes on Jesus, the champion who initiates and perfects our faith. Because of the joy awaiting him, he endured the cross, disregarding its shame … Think of all the hostility he endured from sinful people; then you won't become weary and give up.
Hebrews 12:1–3

Don't copy the behavior and customs of this world, but let God transform you into a new person by changing the way you think.
Romans 12:2

I press on to possess that perfection for which
Christ Jesus first possessed me.
Philippians 3:12

~~~~~

One may see life as a "rat race," or more positively, and with greater fruit, see it as a race for excellence in Christ. The race passes through changing terrain, and goes over hills and through valleys. But if we falter occasionally, Jesus, our coach and fan club, continues to cheer us on from the sidelines. He stands along the way, offering refreshing water and emotional uplifting.

He coaches us on the basis of the disciplines that were required in his own successful race while living on earth as the Son of Man. His death and resurrection ensured all who trust in his coaching joyful, eternal life with him.

We begin life in Christ with inborn attitudes, which may hamper us and must be replaced with more productive thoughts. The goal is to imitate Jesus and take on his perfection in our minds and spirits. We are made more and more like the Lord as we are changed into his glorious image.[17]

Christ makes his home in our hearts,[18] and empowers us. The crown that is our prize at the end of the race reflects his glory.[19]

We may be almost to the point of "hitting the wall," a runner's name for short-term discouragement due to effort and fatigue. But "take a new grip with your tired hands and strengthen your weak knees."[20]

Jesus, who initiates and perfects our faith, will renew our energy. The prophet, Isaiah, reassures us: "The Lord is the everlasting God ... He never grows weak or weary ... He gives power to the weak and strength to the powerless. Even youths will become weak and tired, and young men will fall in exhaustion. But those who trust in the Lord will find new strength. They will soar high on wings like eagles. They will run and not grow weary. They will walk and not faint."[21]

# TRUST

# He Does Not Sleep

He will not let you stumble; the one who watches over
you will not slumber. Indeed, he who watches over Israel
never slumbers or sleeps … The Lord keeps watch over
you as you come and go, both now and forever.
Psalm 121:3–4, 8

Jesus said, "Come to me, all of you who are weary and
carry heavy burdens and I will give you rest."
Matthew 11:28

~ ~ ~ ~ ~

Sometimes I ask, when I feel lost,
"Where are you, Lord? Your presence hides."
The answer comes, softly spoken,
"My presence never left your side.

"I dwell within, give you strength,
Bring you hope, buoy up your faith.
I hear your prayer, open doors—
You'll find the answers that you seek.

"My love for you never wanes;
Tune your desires to my caring heart.
I'll guide your steps, light your path;
I'll straighten the road on which you walk.

"As you continue your journey of faith,
You'll know the joy of trust in me.
When in distress you sought my help,
I had a plan to share with you.

"So do not worry when all seems dark;
Cast your burdens at my feet.
I tarry not, nor do I sleep—
I'm always here, close by your side."

# Trust

When I am afraid, I will put my trust in you. I praise
God for what he has promised. I trust in God, so why
should I be afraid? What can mere mortals do to me?
Psalm 56:3–4

Commit everything you do to the Lord. Trust him
and he will help you ... Be still in the presence of
the Lord, and wait patiently for him to act.
Psalm 37:5, 7

Trust in the Lord with all your heart; do not
depend on your own understanding.
Proverbs 3:5

O Lord, you alone are my hope. I've trusted you, O Lord, from
childhood. Yes, you have been with me from birth; from my mother's
womb you have cared for me. No wonder I am always praising you!
Psalm 71:6

~~~~~

Trust in God is to have confidence in his qualities of goodness, love, faithfulness, and strength. For a child, it is to know that Mommy will not abandon her. It is sensing a love that goes far beyond the ordinary. Our faith matures as we learn to trust in our Lord and Savior, Jesus Christ, whose love cannot be comprehended.

Trust, based on love, is without fear.[22] There is no doubt in the strength and sufficiency of the God we love. The Lord delights in our trust and prayers,[23] and in those whose joy is in doing his will because his instructions are written on their hearts.[24]

When our relationships with Christ are nurtured daily, we will think of him first in any need, large or small. His names are many: counselor, shepherd, guide, and light; the way, truth, and life; bread and water of life, the word, savior, Lord, and many more. Each one describes a way in which he relates to us. There is no lack of his resources in any dilemma or trial when we live in him.

He is delighted when we turn to him in all circumstances. The Spirit of Jesus dwells within each believer and is able to provide an answer even as a question is being asked.[25] Further, our Father in heaven knows our needs before we ask.[26]

Prayer activates the response of God. This may have happened at a time when my young grandson fell off a skateboard, seriously injuring his arm. He was in great pain and was frightened. His parents were on their way home when he fell. They gave a few instructions by phone to his sisters and quickly returned home, praying for the best.

At home, he was sitting down in great distress and supporting his arm, which appeared to be broken. His dad, a physician, splinted it and made him as comfortable as possible. But when X-rays revealed the true injury, it was a simple green-stick fracture, which healed quickly.

One cannot know what the outcome would have been without prayer. If nothing else, it provided comfort and confidence to a young boy in the midst of fear, trauma, and pain. But a contemporary proverb might state, "If in doubt, pray." Without prayer, opportunities to glorify God would not happen.[27]

Prayer for protection from the worst possibilities can strengthen trust. The psalmist declares, "[The Lord] alone is my refuge, my place of safety; he is my God and I trust him … He will cover you with his feathers. He will shelter you with his wings. His faithful promises are your armor and protection."[28] In difficult times, prayer may not keep us out of the dark valley. But we need not fear, for the Lord is close beside us. The "wings of prayer" carry us *through* the valley and the goodness and unfailing love of the Lord will pursue us throughout our lives.[29]

# Great Is Your Faithfulness

Great is God's faithfulness; his mercies begin afresh each morning.
Lamentations 3:22

Your unfailing love, O Lord, is as vast as the heavens;
your faithfulness reaches beyond the clouds.
Psalm 36:5

It is good to proclaim your unfailing love in the morning,
your faithfulness in the evening ... Your faithfulness
extends to every generation, as enduring as the earth you
created ... Hear my prayer, O Lord; listen to my plea!
Answer me because you are faithful and righteous.
Psalm 92:2; Psalm 119:90; Psalm 143:1

~ ~ ~ ~ ~

Sunflowers are known for their tendency to follow the path of the sun. It is not unlike the need for us to focus on the Son, Jesus, to bring discipline and order into our relationship with him.

Sunflowers that are grown for their seeds usually tower over other plants. The prominent flower on top may grow until it is twelve inches or more in diameter. It is a magnificent plant whose seeds provide a source of food for insects, birds, small animals, and people.

The flowers of this plant follow the path of the sun across the sky from east to west. In this way, they receive the full benefits of the sunshine streaming onto their "faces," gathering as much light as possible to promote the process of photosynthesis, by which they produce the food components that nourish them. The sunlight also warms the flowers to help them attract the notice of insects, which are necessary to pollinate them so seeds will form.

The buds of the plant, until they become too heavy as maturing flowers, are the only part of the plant that turns from east to west by means of processes within the stem. As the stem stiffens to support their weight, they are no longer able to turn.

When the new day begins, whether the sun is hidden by clouds or shining from a clear blue sky, the flower head has already turned to face the sun. It is not clear how this happens, but a unique capability within the plant is apparently at work during the darkness. It seems to be triggered as the darkness of the night gives way to gradually returning daylight hours.

Several concepts may be pointed out from the natural actions of the sunflower.

First, they innately focus on the source of their strength for their ability to produce substances necessary for growth, and to form fruit.

The fruit that we produce is in the good things God planned for us before we were born.[30]

Second, sunflowers, warmed by the sun, attract the pollinating insects necessary to perpetuate their lives.

Our spirits, warmed by the love of our faithful God, respond by growing in maturity.

Third, they adapt to influences inherent in their growth. When it becomes desirable for their stems to gain strength by becoming more rigid, they respond to poorly understood signals within the plant.

Often during the course of our lives, events happen that require us to seek God for new direction and adapt our lives accordingly, with thankfulness in all circumstances.[31] As we follow his guidance, he keeps us faithful and strong in our walk with him. Seeking and receiving guidance, or "hearing" God speak to us in any of many ways, is a mysterious gift.

Fourth, the plant will be stunted if it is growing in a shady area. But with adequate light, the plant grows straight and sturdy. The stem is difficult to break into sections on a fully mature sunflower.

Similarly, if we do not put our wholehearted trust in Christ, our light, we will not be able to fulfill the potential that is unique to each of us. We can do everything through Christ who strengthens us.[32]

And, finally, given the elements necessary for growth, we, too, will become like bright, eye-catching sunflowers. We will be examples who draw others to Jesus Christ through the light of the Holy Spirit who dwells within and gives us a message for the world.

Great is his faithfulness!

# JOY

# Joy in the Morning

Let me hear of your unfailing love each morning, for I am
trusting you. Show me where to walk, for I give myself to
you …Teach me to do your will, for you are my God. May
your gracious Spirit lead me forward on a firm footing.
Psalm 143:8, 10

You placed the world on its foundation so it would never be moved
… Mountains rose and valleys sank to the levels you decreed … You
made the moon to mark the seasons, and the sun knows when to set.
Psalm 104:5, 8, 19

~~~~~

As I awake to an untouched day,
I praise my God for his gracious love.
Gazing out at the pristine morning,
I delight in the vista greeting my eyes
That was planned before time began.

By the word of the sovereign living God,
All was spoken into place.
Land and sea, nature's wonders,
Forests and prairies, mountains and canyons;
His hand is present in everything.

Birds chirp with joy as darkness is vanquished,
A cheerful start that shapes my day.
Sunrise follows with pastel-hued sky.
Seasons greet me, one by one,
Each with a flavor of its own.

Flowers spring forth after a long, cold winter;
Summer slips in with warmth and color.
The earth is transformed with autumn's colors;
Winter arrives with frosty breath.
God's faithful order maintains the earth.

Children play with no restraint—
A precious freedom born of the Spirit.
Jesus came to bring that freedom
To all who trust their lives to him,
Who come with a child's innocent values.

Seeing life through the eyes of a child
Gives special joy to brighten each day.
The world is renewed; mystery abounds,
Awaiting the freshness of an open mind
To worship the Author of all I see.

# The Joy of the Lord

We pray that you will be strengthened with all his glorious
power so you will have all the endurance and patience you
need. May you be filled with joy, always thanking the Father.
Colossians 1:11–12

When troubles come your way, consider it an opportunity for great
joy. For you know that when your faith is tested, your endurance
has a chance to grow. So let it grow, for when your endurance is fully
developed, you will be perfect and complete, needing nothing.
James 1:2–4

… Let us run with perseverance the race marked out for us.
Let us fix our eyes on Jesus, the author and perfecter of our
faith, who for the joy set before him endured the cross.
Hebrews 12:1–3 (NIV)

Always be full of joy in the Lord. I say it again–rejoice!
Philippians 4:4

~ ~ ~ ~ ~

There is a subtle difference between the words "happy" and "joyful". To
be happy is to feel or show pleasure or contentment.

"Joy," especially as used in the Bible, represents feelings of great happiness,
pleasure, or contentment, especially of a spiritual kind. It is a fruit of the
Holy Spirit and is rooted in Jesus Christ. It is not dependent on where
we live, or on how much we possess. We trust the Lord to provide our
basic material needs.

Happiness depends on circumstances, on wants fulfilled, or on events
going according to our plans. If one's relationship with the Lord is not
secure and unshakeable, it is difficult to be content with very little.

Millions of Christians worldwide have few possessions and little security, or may suffer for their faith. But their joy in their salvation and freedom in Christ overflows, even when oppressed, deprived of material things, or imprisoned for their faith.

My daughter experienced this attitude when she studied for a few months in Central America. During that time, the students performed works of service. They were hosted in the homes of people who lived in the area. Their dwellings were of simple construction, with packed earth floors. The cooking stoves were located outside, and there was no electricity or running water.

In the home that welcomed my daughter, the grandmother awoke at 4:00 a.m. and prayed aloud. The families had never known any other lifestyle and were content with their simple lives. Their joy in worship—during two hour-long services—was unsurpassed.

The students, like many others who have lived in similar circumstances among people who have little but are content, came home with a new understanding of the relative value of many things we take for granted.

In Haiti, immediately after the earthquake in January, 2010, the wonderful, joyous spirit of the people was also demonstrated. After the earthquake, they worshipped with great joy in what was left of their churches. They had lost almost everything. Their homes were crushed beyond repair; many suffered serious injury including loss of limbs; loved family members and friends were missing. They didn't know where their next meals, or even drinks of safe water, would come from. But they still had life, such as it was, and they worshipped God with thanksgiving and great joy.

Joy has another quality that happiness may lack. A person who is happy is usually content. But a joyful person tends to glow in his or her personality with a light given by the indwelling Holy Spirit. It cannot be faked. One may appear happy in his or her circumstances. But joy is an exuberant gift of the Lord that persists in spite of circumstances. It is evident in the eyes and body language of a person filled with joy.

If one is joyful, his or her spirit can triumph in any circumstance.

# GUIDANCE

# Treasure Map

For where your treasure is, there your heart will be also.
Matthew 6:21

The commandments of the Lord are right, bringing joy to the
heart. The commands of the Lord are clear, giving insight for
living … They are more desirable than gold, even the finest gold.
Psalm 19:8, 10

I am the bread of life. Whoever comes to me will never be
hungry again. Whoever believes in me will never be thirsty.
John 6:35

~~~~~

The day is young when I arise—
      a treasure lies in wait for me.
I make haste to find its source
      so that its beauty I may see.

The map I use is very old;
      its clues are there for each to find.
But first I need to meet my guide—
      this treasure is not the earthly kind.

I open my heart, greet him by name;
      his name is Jesus; I call him Lord.
We do not tarry, but set right to work
      to seek out treasure in his holy word.

I read the book with a sense of awe
      at the precious nuggets before my eyes;
A mine so rich, it has no end—
      my spirit is fed by this bread of life.

And so begins my daily quest;
        my guide is always there to lead.
In his book is an endless source
        of truth that lies in wait for me.

These precious nuggets I safely store
        in my heart and in my mind;
And though I seek my whole life long,
        I know there'll always be more to find.

# The Path Chosen

Acknowledge that the Lord is God! He made us, and we
are his. We are his people, the sheep of his pasture.
Psalm 100:3

Look! I stand at the door and knock. If you hear my voice and open
the door, I will come in, and we will share a meal together as friends.
Revelation 3:20

~ ~ ~ ~ ~

"I'm in control," I told myself.
Ignoring the claim of God on my life,
I forged ahead on a self-chosen path,
Blind to signs that warned of strife.

Life seemed good, all desires met;
But "good" turned out to be a lie.
In despair, I turned to God,
Asked his help with a long, deep sigh.

A sudden breeze rustled leaves;
On the breath of air, I sensed a voice:
"Look within your heart, my child—
I've been waiting for a change of choice."

A light clicked on within my soul;
Objections quickly melted away.
A narrow path to the side appeared;
The light of Christ lit my way.

In my relief, I turned to him;
Jesus thought no less of me.
His love had kept me safe thus far;
From chains of sin, I was now free.

Jesus will never pass us by
Though our backs to him are turned.
He gives us eyes of faith to see
The path that many choose to spurn.

Gently, he knocked on the door of my heart;
I opened it wide, invited him in.
I firmly closed the door to self;
My life is now secure in him.

# BLAMELESS

## in

## CHRIST

# White as Snow

Though your sins are like scarlet, they shall be as white as snow.
Though they are red like crimson, they shall be as wool.
Isaiah 1:18 (NKJV)


[God] has reconciled you to himself through the death
of Christ in his physical body. As a result, he has brought
you into his own presence, and you are holy and blameless
as you stand before him without a single fault.
Colossians 1:22


~ ~ ~ ~ ~


Snowflakes fell while I slept;
They softly covered all the ground.
Everywhere was still and white;
Not a flaw could be found.

In holy stillness long ago,
A child was born during the night.
While most folks slept, angels sang
Praises to God, who had sent men light.

They told of one whose task would be
God's truth and love to men to show.
He shed his blood for all on earth
To wash our sins as white as snow.

How can I, then, deny the one
Who gave his life to set me free?
Gladly to him my life I give
To serve where he leads, joyfully.

# Dust Motes

Why do you look at the speck that is in your brother's eye,
but do not notice the log that is in your own eye?
Matthew 7:3 (NASB)

May you always be filled with the fruit of your salvation—the
righteous character produced in your life by Jesus Christ.
Philippians 1:11

Pursue righteous living, faithfulness, love, and peace.
II Timothy 2:22

~ ~ ~ ~ ~

Dust is found almost everywhere. In our homes, it settles in layers and floats in the air. It may also be seen in an immaterial way as unrighteous thoughts. Spiritually, the heart is the repository of righteous and unrighteous thoughts and motivations.

Floating dust specks, or "motes" as the King James Bible calls them, are easily seen in an open space when a shaft of light shines through their midst. In Matthew 7:3, the speck (mote) in one's eye represents unrighteous actions and emotions. As we allow the light of truth to penetrate the deepest recesses of our hearts, motes of unrighteousness are exposed to its light. When we pursue righteous living, virtues such as faithfulness, love, and peace will gradually mark our lives. Proverbs 4:18 tells us, "The way of the righteous is like the first gleam of dawn, which shines ever brighter until the full light of day."

Jesus taught, often by parables, about how to be right with God. He demonstrated the faithfulness of God's love for us as in the parable of the prodigal son, which emphasized the love of his father that never changed as he waited and watched for his son to repent and return. He introduced the new era which replaced the old, prophesized by the Old Testament prophet, Jeremiah, when the words of the Lord would be written on the hearts of his people, effectively governing their lives from within.[33]

As dust motes of unrighteousness are exposed and swept away, our spirits begin to radiate the light of Christ to those around us. We use our whole body to do what is right for the glory of God.[34] We leave the old way behind in a "cloud of dust" as the Spirit of Christ renews our life.

# A LIGHT

## in the

# DARKNESS

# Jesus, the Ultimate Light

In the beginning the Word already existed. The Word was with God, and the Word was God ... The Word gave life to everything that was created and his life brought light to everyone. The light shines in the darkness, and the darkness can never extinguish it.
John 1:1, 4–5

I am the light of the world. If you follow me, you won't have to walk in darkness because you will have the light that leads to life.
John 8:12

Your word is a lamp to guide my feet and a light for my path.
Psalm 119:5

~~~~~

Life is an adventure that asks this question: "What will we do with the gifts and abilities that we are given?" It begins with total dependence on someone who will meet our daily needs. As we grow, we assert independence and often proclaim, as a two-year-old child may, "I can do it by myself."

As we grow in understanding, we are required to make choices, some of which will determine the courses of our lives, such as who our friends are, our lifestyles, and the work we do. Some hold a lifetime of challenge, some have few surprises, and others are marked "proceed at your own risk."

Jesus Christ came to seek and save those who are lost.[35] His love was "real love—not that we loved God, but that he loved us and sent his Son as a sacrifice to take away our sins."[36] He asks only that we entrust our lives to him in love and believe in his sufficiency. We do not need to earn his love; it is a free gift. The quality of the good works we do in his service is of greater importance than how much we do.

Each of us has been given good works to do.[37] Some people are dependent on others because of their health or limitations. But their lives are of value in the eyes of God. Those who are able may be given the gift of helping those less capable. The helpless may be a gift in themselves as their dependence enriches the lives of those who give of themselves in Christ.

No matter whether we are the helped or the helpless, the light of Christ shines through us as we give all we are, and will become, to the best of our abilities to the one who lights our paths.

# Aglow with the Spirit

If you are filled with light, with no dark corners, then your whole life
will be radiant, as though a floodlight were filling you with light.
Luke 11:36

Live clean, innocent lives as children of God, shining like
bright lights in a world full of crooked and perverse people.
Philippians 2:15

Never lag in zeal and in earnest endeavor; be aglow
and burning with the Spirit, serving the Lord.
Romans 12:11 (Amp.)

~~~~~

As a child, I would go outside early in the evening and capture fireflies. Evenings were enchanting, as the tiny insects danced in the air, flashing their lights. I loved carrying their enchantment within a jar back inside with me, where I placed the jar beside my bed and watched them flicker as I fell asleep. In the morning, they were released, having fulfilled their purpose of creating wonder in a child's mind.

Fireflies produce a "cold light" in a specialized organ, which enables a chemical reaction that creates light. The immature form, the caterpillar-like larvae, sometimes called glowworms, may also produce light. They overwinter underground, or under protective covering, emerging as adults in the spring. Bad taste and sometimes a poisonous toxin protect them from becoming a meal.

No less mysterious than this light created in the small bodies of fireflies, and some other small animals who survive in the darkness of caves or deep in the ocean where light never penetrates, is the light produced in men and women indwelt by the Spirit of God.

The light that radiates from us is not cold and chemically produced. It has warmth to it, a glow that reflects the love of Jesus. Others are attracted to it, especially those who are also "children of God." This light is a radiant "attitude" composed of love, compassion, empathy, and service in Jesus's name.

We can become beacons of light wherever we live. Just as the flashing light of a firefly attracts notice, so our demeanors, attitudes, love, and acts of service set us apart in a world that is "full of crooked and perverse people." But there is good news in Christ. He is "the light [that] shines in the darkness, and the darkness can never extinguish it.[38] Though the powers of darkness continue to resist God,[39] "every child of God defeats this evil world, and we achieve this victory through our faith"[40] in Christ Jesus, who has overcome the world.[41]

# FREEDOM

## in

## CHRIST

# Freedom of the Spirit

The heavens proclaim the glory of God. The skies display his craftsmanship. Day after day they continue to speak; night after night they make him known. They speak without a sound or word; their voice is never heard. Yet their message has gone throughout the earth.
Psalm 19:1–4

When he comes, he will open the eyes of the
blind and unplug the ears of the deaf.
Isaiah 35:5

…You [the Lord's Chosen Servant, Jesus] will be a
light to guide the nations. You will free the [spiritual]
captives from prison [a prison of sin].
Isaiah 42:6–7

Jesus told him, "I am the way, the truth, and the life. No
one can come to the Father except through me."
John 14:16

If the Son sets you free, you are truly free.
John 8:36

~~~~~

Visible threads of the glory of God
Weave through the darkness of the midnight sky;
The heavens reveal his marvelous works.
Wonder and awe flood my spirit
At the glory displayed before my eyes—
My spirit overflows with words of praise.

His abundant love embraces the nations;
He longs for all to seek his face.
But the noisy allure of many distractions
Deafens the ears of some who wander,
And many are blind to the evidence
Found in the silent evening sky.

The saving message of God's grace
Has come to earth as Son of Man.
Through his Spirit who dwells within,
Ordinary followers beacons become.
They are dots of light around the earth
Connected by a magnificent truth.

God's love takes in all peoples on earth.
Those who wander in darkness dense
Are never far from a dot of light
Who prays faithfully day by day
That they may listen and come to know
The Truth who yearns to set them free.

The chains that bind and imprison their spirits,
Preventing fullness of life in Christ,
Will fall away in the breath of a prayer.
In coming to know the living God,
Their spirits find a resting place
And freedom the darkness cannot breach.

Freedom in Christ brings great joy;
No trials or burdens can take it away.
No efforts of those who deny Christ's name
Can touch a spirit united with his.
Those who suffer for their faith
Possess a freedom they cannot lose.

# SPREADING

## the

## GOOD NEWS

# Ripples

The rain and snow come down from the heavens and stay on the ground to water the earth. They cause the grain to grow, producing seed for the farmer and bread for the hungry. It is the same with my word. I send it out, and it always produces fruit. It will accomplish all I want it to, and it will prosper everywhere I send it.
Isaiah 55:11

~~~~~

I tossed a pebble into a pond;
　　　The day was still, no breeze disturbed
　　　The water's surface, smooth as glass.
From the splash ripples sprang—
　　　They spread in circles, crossed the pond.

The pond is like a pond of life.
　　　As we enter, we make a splash;
　　　The pattern of each is unique.
The ripples spreading from our lives
　　　Will have effects we cannot know.

When we live our lives in love
　　　And Christ is Lord of all we do,
　　　The love of God surfs across the waves.
The ripple begun by one small splash
　　　Will spread his love from shore to shore.

# The Way to Life

There are different kinds of service, but we serve the
same Lord. God works in different ways, but it is
the same God who does the work in all of us.
I Corinthians 12:5–6

Let all that I am wait quietly before God, for my
hope is in him. He alone is my rock and my salvation,
my fortress where I will not be shaken.
Psalm 62:5–6

The Holy Spirit produces this kind of fruit in our lives; love,
joy, peace, patience, kindness, gentleness, and self-control.
Galations 5:22–23

I am leaving you with a gift–peace of mind and heart. And the peace
I give is a gift the world cannot give. So don't be troubled or afraid.
John 15:27

~~~~

At your heart's door, he gently knocks;
He offers life anchored in rock.
No one he calls has talents too few;
There is work for each to do.

In this wide world where sin is rife,
He is the way, the truth, and the life.
He is the source of love and kindness;
He gives us peace of heart and mind.

Heed today his earnest call;
Give him your life, your love, your all.
You'll find riches beyond belief,
But not the kind that causes grief.

His kingdom is like yeast, unseen,
That permeates souls so they will lean
On God the Father, who loves each one.
These are words of Jesus, God's Son.

He humbled himself, became as man;
Accepting death, he fulfilled God's plan.
He lives again, and is exalted now
That at his name, every knee shall bow.

# AN ANCHOR

## for

# OUR FAITH

# Blessed Assurance

So God has given both his promise and his oath. These two
things are unchangeable because it is impossible for God to
lie. Therefore we who have fled to him for refuge can have
great confidence as we hold onto the hope that lies before us.
This hope is a strong and trustworthy anchor for our souls.
Hebrews 6:18–19

Come to me, all of you who are weary and carry
heavy burdens, and I will give you rest.
Matthew 11:28

Jesus Christ is the same yesterday, today, and forever.
Hebrews 13:8

~~~~~

Blessed assurance, words divine,
     Bringing peace to this soul of mine.
Jesus speaks over the sands of time,
     His love transcendent and sublime.
Each day with him is a day well spent;
     Blessed assurance, I'm heaven bent.

Some days bring joy, others pain;
     When living in Christ, nothing's in vain;
I'll trust in him, an anchor sure.
     If all else fails, my ship is moored
To his unchanging, timeless grace
     That reaches, covers, every place.

Life is a voyage each one takes;
How we prepare, a difference makes.
When Christ is Lord, he gives us rest;
He calms the seas; our trip is blessed.
Our ship, though battered, the shore will gain—
Blessed assurance, blessed refrain.

# My Body, a Temple

...Christ's one act of righteousness brings a right relationship
with God and new life for everyone. But because one ... person
obeyed God, many will be made righteous ... So just as sin
ruled over all people and brought them to death, now God's
wonderful grace rules instead, giving us right standing with God
and resulting in eternal life through Jesus Christ our Lord.
Romans 5:18–19, 21

Your body is the temple of the Holy Spirit, who
lives in you and was given to you by God.
II Corinthians 3:18

No one can lay any foundation other than the one we already
have—Jesus Christ. Anyone who builds on that foundation may
use a variety of materials—gold, silver, jewels, wood, hay or straw.
But on the judgment day, fire will reveal what kind of work each
builder has done. The fire will show if a person's work has any value.
I Corinthians 3:11–13

Stay alert! Watch out for your great enemy, the devil. He prowls
around like a roaring lion, looking for someone to devour.
I Peter 5:8

~ ~ ~ ~ ~

The décor and worship furnishings in the temple Solomon built were
of great value. In seeing our bodies as temples, the moral and spiritual
values we nurture through a relationship with Jesus become invaluable
in determining whether our buildings will be of eternal quality.

We must prepare our hearts for the Holy Spirit. He cannot dwell in
them unless they are pure and blameless. The condition of the heart
determines the words and actions of the outer person. We are given the
responsibility of building a life worthy of Christ. Its quality will depend

on the depth of our commitment to him. We must be willing to go all the way, to fulfill our God-given abilities.

The children's story of the three little pigs illustrates in a visual way the different quality of the type of house, or temple, each built. For better scriptural analogy, this story is about three young sheep that set off from home to live on their own. Each one intended to build a house to keep him safe from the dangers of the world.

The first sheep, nicknamed Flash, quickly patched a home together with whatever became available first. It happened to be a stack of straw in an open, unprotected area where no one was authorized to control wild animals or the condition of the surroundings. The animals there all lived independently. It was not a safe area of the woods.

Flash was exhausted when he built the last of the straw into walls and a thatched roof. He went inside to take a nap.

A wily wolf with a dubious reputation, whose name was DeCeive, lived in a brushy place in the woods in a small cave in a hillside. He had been observing Flash and the weakness inherent in his house. DeCeive was hungry and decided to burrow into the heart of Flash's home where he was napping peacefully without regard for any dangers present in the woods.

DeCeive's paws quickly dug out enough straw to make a small hole in the wall. He crawled through and crept silently toward Flash. But before DeCeive could get to him, Flash woke with a start, sensing something was wrong. He leaped up and escaped through his door, running for his life. DeCeive became stuck in the doorway, and Flash found a safe place to hide.

The second sheep, named Folly, was foolish. He did not think things through to possible consequences. He met a man transporting a large load of small branches to be used for firewood. The man questioned Folly about the wisdom of using a material that even woven together lacked both strength and warmth. But Folly persisted. He obtained enough branches to put together a small house, stuffed moss and clay mud into the cracks, and settled in.

DeCeive wandered by, hidden behind bushes. He sidled over to the closed entrance of Folly's house. Knocking on the door, he asked to come in. But he could not disguise his gruff voice, and Folly, shaking with fear, refused to open the door. He braced a chair tightly against it. He had been warned about wolves, even those who seemed friendly. So DeCeive left to gather together some other wolves he knew. They soon returned, and despite Folly's frightened protests, shoved the house over in three attempts. Folly was fortunate to escape with his life.

The third sheep, Solomon, had different values than his brothers. He was wise and worked hard. He learned from the mistakes of others and his own. He had studied how to live a life that pleased the great shepherd, and the qualities that went into a secure home, such as love, integrity, understanding, hospitality, and pride of workmanship. He exhibited a love of all things good, and faith and trust in the great shepherd, who frequently checked up on the sheep in his many flocks and tended to their needs. Folly built his house with bricks, the best money could buy. When it was completed, he stepped inside to enjoy the fruit of his labor.

Soon, DeCeive came by to see if he could scare off Solomon and take over his house. He begged to be let in, promising all sorts of benefits such as power, wealth, and a bigger house. His best talents were deception and misinterpretation. But Solomon had studied the bible for sheep thoroughly and had a truth to counter every lie.[42] He had built his house on a foundation of words of life, and he could not be swayed.

Finally, DeCeive left with his tail between his legs. He hated defeat. He whined to himself that the great shepherd had all the advantages—but he would keep his eyes open for an opportunity to find a weakness in Solomon's armor.[43]

He would find that Solomon was so well grounded in the teachings of the great shepherd that he never would be successful in deceiving him. The words in Solomon's bible were his truth and way of life. The home he constructed would last for eternity.

As children of God, we must choose carefully what we use for building blocks in our temples for the Holy Spirit. The foundation of our lives will be built on words such as these:

"Let your roots grow down into [Christ], and let your lives be built on him. Then your faith will grow strong in the truth you were taught, and you will overflow with thankfulness." Colossians 2:7

"Test everything that is said. Hold on to what is good. Stay away from every kind of evil." I Thessalonians 5:21–22

"Now may the God of peace–who brought up from the dead our Lord Jesus, the great Shepherd of the sheep ... may he equip you with all you need for doing his will. May he produce in you, through the power of Jesus Christ, every good thing that is pleasing to him." Hebrews 13:20–21

# REFLECTION

## and

# MEDITATIONS

# Solitude

[Jesus] went up into the hills by himself to pray.
Matthew 14:23

A person standing alone can be attacked and defeated, but two can
stand back-to-back and conquer. Three are even better, for a triple-
braided cord is not easily broken.
Ecclesiastes 4:12

Just as our bodies have many parts and each part has a special
function, so it is with Christ's body. We are many parts of one body,
and we all belong to each other.
Romans 12:4–5

~~~~~

Who am I when I am alone?

I seek answers to ultimate questions,
          answers that go to the heart of the matter.
My earnest search comes back to me:
How do I fit the facets of my life
          into the community in which I live?
Where is God leading me?
How do I prepare for unknown events
          for which I have no way to plan?

I find answers in God's Word:
          "If you look for me wholeheartedly,
               you will find me."[44]
          "Faith ... gives us assurance about things
               we cannot see."[45]
          "The Lord leads the humble in doing right,
               teaching them his way."[46]

I find answers in fellowship,
      and in the midst of community.
In solitude, I find myself;
      in community, I give myself.
In solitude, I receive
      the blessings of strength and faith;
In community, I am able to share
      the truths I have learned at Jesus's feet.

In community is unity
      as those composing the family of God
      build the holy body of Christ.
Community and solitude
      must exist side by side.
Solitude needs community
      to renew and refresh its resources.
Community needs solitude
      to grow on insights it has been given.

Jesus practiced both in his life;
      times of solitude with his Father
      gave him strength to meet the cross.
In community, he taught his disciples
      to trust and pray and love each other.

In his body, solitude finds wisdom,
      And community encourages growth
So God's people will be complete,
      speaking the truth of Christ in love.

# Reflections

As a face is reflected in water, so the heart reflects the real person.
Proverbs 27:19

We take captive every thought to make it obedient to Christ.
II Corinthians 10:5 (NIV)

~ ~ ~ ~ ~

A face reflected is a very small part
Of the one who peers into a mirror.
What is seen is just skin deep;
Who one is, one's heart reveals.

For character lies within, unseen
Except by action or by words
Proving who one truly is;
They are a mirror reflecting one's soul.

Thoughtful words and caring deeds
Form the character bit by bit.
Character moves from inside out;
The face reflects the heart's intent.

Reflections of an unseen kind
Come from a place deep within—
Questions, doubts, praises, hopes,
Directed to our living God.

The mighty power of God within
Enables thoughts to gain real life,
Changing us and the place we live,
The world beyond; God's work is done.

# Journeys

Is it your wisdom that makes the hawk soar and spread
its wings toward the south? Is it at your command that
the eagle rises to the heights to make its nest?
Job 39:26

Those who trust in the Lord will find new strength.
They will soar high on wings like eagles.
Isaiah 40:31

For a man's ways are in full view of the Lord,
and he examines all his paths.
Proverbs 5:21 (NIV)

People may be right in their own eyes, but
the Lord examines their heart.
Proverbs 21:2

~ ~ ~ ~ ~

Today, the geese flew to the north,
long ribbons trailing in the sky,
undulating on currents of air,
honking with joy at arrival of spring.

How far have they traveled on their journey?
Where will they rest at journey's end?
They know without reasoning,
responding to urgings from within.

God gave me gifts of thought and reflection;
I consider my journey through life:
What is my purpose? Which way do I take?
What can I do that will make a difference?

An answer forms within my heart
    from yearnings sent by the living God;
    he reveals the way as I walk
    step by step in his light.

My journey takes me into his presence,
    reflects the unerring flight of the geese
    to their birthplace where they find rest,
    a place of abundance prepared by God.

# Campfire Reflections

Sometimes, the greatest pleasure is found in simple things, such as in a campfire on a cool, moonlit evening. The peaceful sounds generated by small creatures of the night fill the darkness. The sky is cloudless; no city lights dim the stars. They look like millions of pinpoints of light, twinkling through the night. The moon floats among the clouds, its light casting mysterious shadows. The camper's gaze is transfixed on flickering flames, drawing his or her thoughts inward and upward to the creator of all the wonderful things he or she sees and hears. He or she may even be aware of the presence of the Lord as he or she worships silently and with companions.

~ ~ ~ ~ ~

Let all that I am praise the Lord; with my whole heart,
I will praise his holy name. Let all that I am praise the
Lord; may I never forget the good things he does for me.
He forgives all my sins and heals all my diseases.
Psalm 103:1–3

O Lord, you have examined my heart and know everything
about me … You know my thoughts even when I'm far away
… You know everything I do. You know what I am going to say
even before I say it, Lord. You go before me and follow me. You
place your hand of blessing on my head. Such knowledge is too
wonderful for me, too great for me to understand! I can never
escape from your Spirit! I can never get away from your presence
… Darkness and light are the same to you … How precious are
your thoughts about me, O God. They cannot be numbered.
Psalm 139:1–7, 12, 17

For everyone has sinned; we all fall short of God's glorious
standard. Yet God, with undeserved kindness declares that we
are righteous. He did this through Christ Jesus when he freed
us from the penalty for our sins. For God presented Jesus as

the sacrifice for sin. People are made right with God when they
believe that Jesus sacrificed his life, shedding his blood.
Romans 3:23–25

~~~~~

The crackling fire draws me in;
Chatting, laughing, friendships form.
Toasting marshmallows on glowing embers,
I reflect on the wonder of God's care for me.

I sense his presence in rustling leaves,
In crickets chirping through the night,
In lapping of waves upon the shore,
The splash of water as fish leap high.

God's order is seen in the waning moon,
In the break of dawn as nighttime fades,
In dew that glistens on blades of grass,
In songs of birds as they greet the day.

He created woods and fields and lakes,
Birds and flowers, day and night.
When all was complete, he created people
To care for the world in which they dwell.

I hear and see; I am assured
That God is present everywhere.
He daily cares for all my needs,
Knows my feelings and what I think.

God's love and care sent us Jesus,
Who lived his life midst ordinary people.
Out of love he gave his life,
Then rose triumphant over sin and death.

God's plan is clear in retrospect;
He made a way to enter his presence.
Relations restored between God and his people;
Jesus paid the price to make us whole.

# Reflection on Time

For a thousand years in your sight are like a day that has just gone by.
Psalm 90:4

When the right time came, God sent his Son, born of a woman.
Galations 4:4

We can rejoice, too, when we run into problems and trials, for
we know that they help us develop endurance. And endurance
develops strength of character, and character strengthens our
confident hope of salvation. And this hope will not lead to
disappointment. For we know how dearly God loves us, because
he has given us the Holy Spirit to fill our hearts with his love.
Romans 5:3–5

We know that God causes everything to work together for
the good of those who love God and are called according to
his purpose for them. For God knew his people in advance,
and he chose them to become like his Son, so that his Son
would be the first–born among many brothers and sisters.
Romans 8:28

~~~~~

Time is relative in the mind of God,
Speeding like lightning across the sky;
To us, it crawls at the pace of a snail.

Our lives may change with lightning speed,
By random chance, or so it seems—
Bringing to us good times or bad.

God allows trials to open our eyes,
They sharpen discernment to know his voice,
Light a spark within our hearts.

Through the hardships of this life,
God brings good, then better yet;
Our growth in Christ begins to show.

Storms bring purpose to our lives,
Enable God's plan to work for good
As he turns bad upon its head.

With God's perspective on our plight,
We shall sing praises from our hearts
As we embrace his redeeming work.

By humankind's worst, Jesus's life was stilled.
God's mighty power crushed death's grip;
We now enjoy new life in him.

God's time seemed slow to people on earth;
But through the cross, in fullness of time,
The light of Christ was here to stay.

# Perfect Harmony

Praise God in his sanctuary; praise him in his mighty heaven ...
Praise him with the tambourine and dancing; praise him with strings
and flutes ...Let everything that breathes sing praises to the Lord.
Psalm 150:1, 4, 6

Above all, clothe yourselves in love, which binds
us all together in perfect harmony.
Colossians 3:14

We will speak the truth in love, growing in every way more
and more like Christ, who is the head of his body, the church.
He makes the whole body fit together perfectly. As each part
does its own special work, it helps the other parts grow, so that
the whole body is healthy and growing and full of love.
Ephesians 4:15–16

~ ~ ~ ~ ~

Psalm 150, a hymn of praise, names several instruments played together. All of the instruments must be tuned to each other to produce a harmonious melody. If one instrument is not tuned perfectly, disharmony and poor quality of sound result.

A violin, just one kind of stringed instrument used today in worship, is much more than a specially shaped, hollow box with strings. The unique woods that are used in its construction are carefully chosen for age and quality. Many separate small pieces that support and strengthen the body must be shaped out of specific woods. The wood must be aged and finished carefully. The bow is also carefully shaped. Only a master builder who loves his work and cherishes each instrument he builds for its unique qualities can shape a violin with a truly beautiful sound. This sound becomes richer as the instrument is played over many years. In concert, it deepens the quality of the whole.

The body of Christ, the church, is physical in the sense that God's people, indwelt by the Holy Spirit, meet in a particular location, and mostly in a specific building. But there is a universal and spiritual sense when all of God's children over time are included in the heavenly church, Christ's body. The church is "made full and complete by Christ, who fills all things everywhere with himself."[47]

Each member of the body—i.e., each of us—must work together in harmony to do his or her unique part in enabling the church to grow. It is built up in Christ as generations of people each contribute as Jesus leads them. It becomes a richer source of comfort, love, and hope. The church is not one person as one string does not make a violin. It is only built up as each individual contributes to the whole to bring out the harmony and unity found in Christ, who fills all things everywhere with his beauty, peace, and love. In its perfection in Christ, it will send out a greater, ever-expanding witness to the world, drawing others to the message of the good news of the Gospel.

# PRAYER

# Prayer and the Book of Psalms

My God, my God, why have you abandoned me? ... Everyone who
sees me mocks me. They sneer and shake their heads, saying, "Is
this the one who relies on the Lord? Then let the Lord save him! ...
My life is poured out like water, and all my bones are out of joint.
My heart is like wax, melting within me. My strength has dried up
like sunbaked clay. My tongue sticks to the roof of my mouth.
Psalm 22:1, 7–8, 14–15 [A prophecy pointing to Jesus]

Against you and you only have I sinned; I have done what
is evil in your sight ... The sacrifice you desire is a broken
spirit. You will not reject a broken and repentant heart.
Psalm 51:4, 17 [A psalm of David after he had
committed adultery with Bathsheba]

We will not hide these truths [stories our ancestors handed
down to us] from our children; we will tell the next
generation about the glorious deeds of the Lord.
Psalm 78:4 [History recounted]

The Book of Psalms contains ancient prayers and praises of Israel.
They often have musical notations indicating their intent to be used
in worship. Some of them are prophecy pointing to Jesus and their
themes are developed further in the New Testament in Jesus's teaching
and life.

The Psalms are inspired by God through human authors, including
Moses, David, Solomon, and various official musicians. They are diverse
and composed as the responses of God's people to him. Laments, songs
of praise, wisdom, thanksgiving, reflections on God's mighty acts, and
worship are found in them.

The psalms are God–centered. They ask searching questions about
forgiveness for sins; why the godly suffer and the wicked prosper;
suffering and adversity are addressed or questioned. The majority of

the psalms, however, are songs of praise, thanksgiving, prayer, and repentance.[48]

The adversities and questions of the ancient people who wrote the psalms have not changed other than in their nature. The contemporary world has both the same questions, and totally new ones. We, too, experience discouragement, temptation, failure, success, joy, moments of exultation, and a sense of the need to question or praise God.

We, too, find answers in prayer. God knows the human condition. He desires our communication with him concerning all the good and bad times of our lives. He listens and responds according to his wisdom, which is far different from our wisdom. As in Psalm 42:1–3, 11 we long for God in our need:

"As the deer longs for streams of water, so I long for you, O God. I thirst for God, the living God. When can I go and stand before him? Day and night I have only tears for food, while my enemies continually taunt me, saying, "Where is this God of yours?" … I will put my hope in God! I will praise him again—my Savior and my God!

The poems in the Psalms are authentic human expressions of joy and despair, worship and prayer, confession and adoration, and much more. If we are looking for fresh words to communicate with the Lord in prayer, the Psalms are an excellent resource.

# God Hears

I cried out to God for help; I cried out to God to hear
me. When I was in distress, I sought the Lord; at night I
stretched out untiring hands and my soul refused to be
comforted ... I shall remember the deeds of the Lord ... I will
meditate on all your work ...Your way, O God is holy.
Psalm 77:1–2, 11–13

Why am I discouraged? Why is my heart so sad? I will put my
hope in God! I will praise him again—my Savior and my God!
Now I am discouraged, but I will remember you. ... But each
day the Lord pours his unfailing love upon me, and through
each night I sing his songs, praying to God who gives me life.
Psalm 42:5–6

~~~~~

When life becomes too much for me,
When doors seem closed and I cannot see
Beyond the curtain of my despair,
My Father in heaven is always there.

It matters not how well I pray,
Where I am, or what I say;
He knows the burden my spirit bears;
He's never too busy to hear my prayers.

Life is a patchwork that contains
More than burdens, sorrows, and pains.
Laughter and joy are also a part;
Often, I praise him from my heart.

My heart overflows with joy sublime;
My Father in heaven always has time
To hear my prayers of thanksgiving and praise,
Offered to him throughout my days.

# On a Moonlit Night

Be still and know that I am God! I will be honored by every nation.
Psalm 46:10

You are permitted to understand the secrets [literally, "the mysteries"] of the Kingdom of Heaven … To those who listen to my teaching, more understanding will be given, and they will have an abundance of knowledge. But for those who are not listening, even what little understanding they have will be taken from them.
Mt. 13:11–12[49]

~ ~ ~ ~ ~

The evening is peaceful; the wind has calmed;
    The pond before me reflects the stars.
Hidden, secluded, its dark surface still,
    It lies in a hollow surrounded by trees.

This sacred spot is a place for reflection,
    A chapel where my spirit is refreshed.
I glimpse a patch of starlit sky;
    The full moon glows with untold secrets.

A clump of trees forms my shelter,
    Their trunks united at the base.
I settle comfortably into their center,
    A natural chapel where God awaits.

I've stolen away to visit with him
    Here in this quiet, holy niche
Where clouds drift over the rising moon
    And shadows shift in the clearing below.

An owl hoots from a hollow tree;
    Tiny tree frogs, full-throated, sing.

Their bigger cousins, perched on a log,
    Harmonize in deeper tones.

Wild flowers sleep all around;
    Blossoms of some are folded tight.
A raccoon hunts silently for a mouse;
    Fireflies dance, revealed by their lights.

As I reflect on mysteries deep,
    I absorb the peace of this beautiful evening.
A breath of breeze stirs the air;
    I sense the voice of God in my mind.

I still my thoughts, open wide my heart,
    Prepare my spirit to hear his voice.
He whispers, oh, so quietly—
    My spirit rejoices; I give him praise.

In this secluded nook of mine,
    I've found a quiet place to reflect
Where no one comes to break the calm;
    My soul is nourished in the presence of God.

~ ~ ~ ~ ~

This poem is written in memory of a small pond, deep in the woods, surrounded by wildflowers. It was populated by frogs and other creatures, known by no one else. There, God strolled in quietness.

It no longer exists, but fond memories are forever.

# A Thorn Wrapped in Grace

Let all that I am wait quietly for God, for my hope is in him.
He alone is my rock and my salvation, my fortress where I
will not be shaken … O my people, trust in him at all times.
Pour out your heart to him, for God is our refuge.
Psalm 62:5–6, 8

Three different times I begged the Lord to take [the thorn]
away. Each time he said, "My grace is all you need. My power
works best in weakness." So now I am glad to boast about my
weaknesses, so that the power of Christ can work through me.
II Corinthians 12:8–9

~~~~

My spirit feels overwhelmed and distressed;
    My burden has become too heavy to bear.
I look out from behind the bars of my prison;
    My hope has been worn paper thin.
Prayers go nowhere, lost in space;
    Discouragement follows me everywhere.
I paste on a smile, but my eyes are blank.
    Help me, Lord, before I sink—
This thorn has become larger than me.

I fall silent, without words,
    Emotions shattered by overuse.
And then—in my mind—just two words:
    "Trust me," it says, and it is gone.
I say to the voice, "You always say that,"
    When my strength becomes a slender thread.
"I will," I say and sense that voice
    Speaking words more precious than gold:
"My strength is sufficient to carry your load."

Breathing prayers of thanksgiving and praise,
      I know that Jesus never left my side.
Rather, my eyes lost their focus on him
      As realities of pain took their toll.
Turning back to Christ, my rock,
      I anchor my faith, safe and secure.
He fills me with his perfect joy;
      Flooding my spirit, overflowing my heart;
A fountain of love refreshes my soul.

# Love Letter

We know how much God loves us, and we have put our trust in his love. God is love, and all who live in love live in God, and God lives in them. And as we live in God, our love grows more perfect.
I John 4:16–17

I am convinced that nothing can ever separate us from God's love. Neither death nor life ... neither our fears for today nor our worries about tomorrow—not even the powers of hell can separate us from God's love. No power in the sky above or in the earth below–indeed nothing in all creation will ever be able to separate us from the love of God that is revealed in Christ Jesus our Lord.
Romans 8:38–39

If you need wisdom, ask our generous God, and he will give it to you.
James 1:5

God is our refuge and strength, always
ready to help in times of trouble.
Psalm 46:1

~ ~ ~ ~ ~

Dear Jesus,

Why should letters expressing love
    Be only for relationships on earth
When the source of love dwells in the heavens?

When I need you,
    You have already begun to meet my need.
When I suffer,
    You give me power to rejoice in you.
When I am uncertain,
    Your wisdom gives clarity to my mind.

Mistakes committed
     Can never change your love for me.
As I pray,
     Unlimited peace floods my soul.

I know with unshakeable certainty
     That life without you is life without love.
I see your love in everything—
     In beauty of nature, in relationships.
It was your love that carried me
     Through the joys and trials of growing in you.

The path I followed was mine alone;
     It molded and made me who I am.
Or perhaps my life conformed to your guidance
     As opportunities and people crossed my path,
Altering my course at crucial times.

Your loving care is my source of strength;
     My love is limited by human nature.
I give it to you as it is,
     Moment by moment, for you to perfect.
Thank you, Jesus, for loving me
     Unconditionally, as I am.

Your disciple in learning to know your mind,
     A thankful follower learning to love.

# TRIALS

# and

# DIFFICULTIES

# The End of the Rope

This poem comes from an expression that implies one has done everything he or she can, feels out of options, or feels helpless and without hope.

~~~~~

God is our merciful Father and the source of all comfort. He comforts us in all our troubles so that we can comfort others. When they are troubled, we will be able to give them the same comfort God has given us. For the more we suffer for Christ, the more God will shower us with his comfort through Christ.
II Corinthians 1:3–5

[Jesus said], I am telling you nothing but the truth when I say it is profitable (good …) for you that I go away. Because if I do not go away, the Comforter (Counselor, Helper, Advocate, Intercessor, Strengthener, Standby) will not come to you [in close fellowship with you]; but if I go away, I will send him to you [to be in close fellowship with you].
John 16:7 (Amp.)

~~~~~

When troubles surround and fill your days,
When the sky seems dark and rain pours down,
When all seems lost, with nowhere to turn,
And you feel you've reached the end of your rope—
Call on Jesus,
     He will give you hope.

His light will pierce the darkness ahead.
Trials and clouds are allowed by God;
He lines them with silver, makes them a source
Of his incomparable strength, claimed by faith,
When it seems we've come
      To the end of our ropes.

Patience, persistence—character comes next;
Our spirits mature through suffering and pain.
Our perspectives widen to the larger world
Where pain is rampant, unrelieved—
We extend ropes
      To others in need.

Christ, our anchor, secures the rope.
God's desire is comfort for all—
The Spirit of God who resides within
Guides, enables as we reach out
To pass along
      Comfort and hope.

# Safely through the Storm

"Lord, help!" they cried in their trouble, and he saved them from
their distress. He calmed the storm to a whisper and stilled the waves.
Psalm 107:28–29

When I came to the city of Troas to preach the Good News
of Christ, the Lord opened a door of opportunity for me.
II Corinthians 3:12

I know that our lives are not our own. We are not able to plan
our own course. So correct me, Lord, but please be gentle.
Jeremiah 10:23–24

The Lord directs the steps of the godly. He delights in
every detail of their lives. Though they stumble, they will
never fall, for the Lord holds them by the hand.
Psalm 37:23–24

~~~~~

We are driving toward a threatening sky. Suddenly, enormous drops
of rain are plopping noisily onto the windshield, obscuring the road
ahead; we quickly turn on the windshield wipers. The intensity of the
rain pouring down increases rapidly until sheets of water wash across
the car. All we can see on the road ahead is a sheet of water; we cannot
see the guiding lines painted on the concrete. We strain to identify the
shoulder of the road. We fear stopping because a car behind might not
see us in time to stop.

Lightning flashes down to the earth in long, jagged streaks; thunder
crashes across the dark sky. The storm is being driven by powerful winds
from the west; it is bigger than the cars in its path. The skies are black
before us.

At last, we are able to turn off the highway onto city streets. Torrents
of water, curb deep, rush down the roadway. Sheets of rain are driven

across the streets and intersections. Water races past the flooded storm sewers. Excess water sprays out of them like small fountains. The force of the storm is incredible. To go around a corner, we are forced by deep water to swing out as we slowly negotiate the turn.

Cars stall in the ponds that spread over the curb, across sidewalks and deep into lawns. Neighbors, standing thigh deep in water, help push them off the street.

Sirens wail in the semi-darkness, warning of a tornado sighting. I pray that the rain might let up enough to allow us to get out of the car at our destination—a somewhat frivolous prayer. But once before, the clouds parted when I prayed for friends who had to get off a bus and walk a mile through heavy rain. They had observed through its windows that they were going to get soaked through; as they departed the bus, the rain slowed to a sprinkle. They described it as "a hole opening up in the clouds."

A few minutes later, the downpour suddenly lessens to light rain. But we can't get through the streets to where we want to go. Two blocks before, the water is too deep to risk driving though it. Several cars that make attempts are stranded in the ponds of water.

We wait a short time and then decide to drive around and approach the house from the opposite direction. Our path leads directly into unforeseen difficulties. We have no choice but to stay on course. As we inch along, a fallen tree limb blocks the path. Flood waters halt our progress, and we make a detour. The difficulties seem endless. By the time we arrive, ten or fifteen minutes after our initial attempt, the water is receding, and the street has drained.

Our Christian experience can include times of smooth traveling. But sometimes, storm clouds rise, replacing the fluffy white piles of clouds resembling cotton candy and the sun that had shone brightly on us.

We know God is leading us, closing one door and opening another. Our vision of what lies ahead is dim. Trusting him, we continue to seek direction. Gradually, the storm moves out of our lives, and the way ahead is clear.

We observe the brightening sky. A rainbow divides the darker sky from the lightened part. It is a double rainbow. Christ, our light, has faithfully guided us through. We successfully negotiated the detour, avoided the pitfalls of deep water, were safely guided and protected through the darkness of the storm. Calm follows in its wake. We join spontaneous fellowship among friends. The air, cleaned of pollutants, smells fresh. We feel renewed.

The next morning, we greet the sunshine with joy. We have been given safe passage yet again. God is good. We know we can depend on him without reservation. He never leaves our side, accompanying us all the way to our eternal destination through countless storms by his guiding presence within.

# Rain in the Desert

I will make a pathway through the wilderness. I will
create rivers in the dry wasteland … so my chosen people
can be refreshed. I have made Israel for myself, and they
will someday honor me before the whole world.
Isaiah 43:19–21

The rain and snow come down from the heavens and stay on
the ground to water the earth. They cause the grain to grow,
producing seed for the farmer and bread for the hungry. It is the
same with my word. I send it out, and it always produces fruit.
Isaiah 55:10–11

"For I know the plans I have for you," says the Lord. "They are
plans for good and not for disaster, to give you a future and a
hope … If you look for me wholeheartedly, you will find me."
Jeremiah 29:11, 13

I will never leave you nor forsake you.
Joshua 1:5 (NIV)

~ ~ ~ ~ ~

Parched, cracked earth welcomed the rain;
A garden of flowers transformed the land
In a rainbow of colors delighting the eye.
As they faded in the scorching sun,
Their ebbing life was preserved in seeds.

Life at times resembles a desert
As God allows his children to walk
Through rock-strewn places for a time.
While seeking the loving face of God,
Seeds of truth form deep in their hearts.

One day, they reach the further side.
The truth they've nurtured faithfully
Takes root in fertile soil there.
It flowers in their daily lives,
A transforming force, Holy Spirit given.

A time of trial may be long or short.
But the presence of God never leaves;
His love protects; He leads the way.
Trusting him to provide our needs
Brings peace and joy wherever we are.

# A Gold-Rimmed Cup

Don't worry about tomorrow, for tomorrow will bring its
own worries. Today's trouble is enough for today.
Matthew 6:34

[Jesus prayed in agony of spirit,] "My Father! If this cup
cannot be taken away unless I drink it, your will be done."
Matthew 26:42

Always be joyful. Never stop praying. Be thankful
in all circumstances, for this is God's will for
you who belong to Christ Jesus.
I Thessalonians 5:16–18

Do not quench (suppress or subdue) the [Holy] Spirit.
I Thessalonians 5:19 (Amp.)

Even though the fig trees have no blossoms, and there are no grapes
on the vines, even though the olive crop fails, and the fields lie
empty and barren; … yet I will rejoice in the Lord! I will be joyful
in the God of my salvation. The sovereign Lord is my strength.
Habakkuk 3:17–19

~~~~~

Joy and suffering are not incompatible. Jesus foretold trials and suffering
for those who followed him. In the western world, we sometimes hear a
prosperity gospel that leads some to expect health, happiness, sufficient
material benefits and stability almost as a right, or an entitlement.
We may read the promises of God and think, "It says right here that
obedience to God will bring us his protection and fulfill our needs."

We may even lean toward this treacherous, judgmental, self-righteous
attitude: "If he or she did not have something sinful in his or life, there
would not be so much suffering in his or her life."

Psalm 73 is an example of conflicting attitudes about the suffering of the righteous, while the wicked prosper. The psalmist felt it should be the other way around. He says, "I envied the proud when I saw them prosper despite their wickedness. They seem to live such painless lives; their bodies are healthy and strong. They don't have troubles like other people" (Psalm 73:3–5). "Did I keep my heart pure for nothing? Did I keep myself innocent for no reason? I get nothing but trouble all day long; every morning brings me pain" (Vs. 13–14) ... "My health may fail, and my spirit may grow weak, but God remains the strength of my heart; he is mine forever" (Vs. 25–27).

All of the apostles except John, who was exiled near the end of his life on the Greek island of Patmos, died violent deaths. Were they happy? Yes, but "happy" falls far short of their true states of mind. They were joyful, exultant, and full of hope, eager to spread the good news that Jesus Christ was all sufficient in this life.

Many of us suffer in our earthly lives for any one of countless reasons. Many search endlessly for fulfillment. Multitudes have found it in Jesus Christ.

In his book, *Prayer: Does It Make Any Difference?*, Philip Yancy asks,

> "Why is suffering distributed so unevenly and unfairly? ... For a time, God has chosen to operate on this broken planet mostly from the bottom up rather than the top down—a pattern God's own Son subjected himself to while on earth. Partly out of respect for human freedom, God often allows things to play out "naturally.""[50]

> "[Jesus] understood that redemption comes from passing through the pain, not avoiding it: "for the joy set before him [he] endured the cross." Somehow redeemed suffering is better than no suffering at all. How remote [this redemptive pattern] seems to all of us in the midst of trials."[51]

In the hilltops and valleys of life, we find strength in the implied word "despite" in the counsel offered in the scriptures that address valleys. It points to the one person (Jesus) who speaks from his dwelling place within our hearts. He embodies the qualities of character described when trials come. Consider the following verses:

> "I have told you all this so that you may have peace in me [despite] the many trials and sorrows [you will have on earth.] But take heart, because I have overcome the world."[52]

> "We can rejoice [despite] problems and trials, for we know that they help us develop endurance. And endurance develops strength of character, and character strengthens our confident hope of salvation".[53]

There is a glorious upside, the silver lining of the cloud for those who persevere through trials for the glory of God. When we put the years of our lives in perspective against the life we will enjoy with Jesus in eternity, we perceive that in God's time, we are on earth for an instant. But the work we do for Christ while we are here and the quality of life we model may have eternal significance in the lives of those around us. In accomplishing our individualized missions on earth, we are given sufficient spiritual strength for anything we may experience. Paul tells us, "Fan into flames the spiritual gift God gave you."[54] That is, cultivate it, or them, if we are given a combination of gifts.

No gift is of any use if it is kept on a shelf. There, it gathers dust and loses its luster, becomes outdated and useless, or deteriorates into dust. The value of a gift lies in multiplying it over and over by its application. The music of the gifted, the comfort of kind words, the wise use of our wealth, the giving of our selves—these enrich our lives and the lives of those who benefit by our ministrations.

The spiritual life is nurtured in the inner person and is greater than any circumstances we may encounter, including death. In eternity, without the burden of a body that breaks down eventually, promises that are broken, expectations dashed, and betrayal, we will thrive to the extent we have nurtured our inner lives.[55]

For a follower of Christ, the spiritual overrules the material in value. Paul, the apostle, suffered greatly, yet he writes, "Not that I was ever in need, for I have learned to be content with whatever I have. I know how to live on almost nothing or with everything. I have learned the secret of living in every situation."[56]

To rejoice through trials may begin by claiming the Lord's strength and offering praise and thanksgiving for the purifying work that is blessing us. Initially, our words may be less than sincere when we are beset by problems or pain. But with time, our prayers become more genuine. Eventually, we find we are able to rejoice through our difficulties.

Life challenges us to overcome and to be the best we can be in Christ. If we walk close to him, we will pass through shadowed valleys of suffering triumphantly with our spirits untarnished and shining bright.

# GROWTH in CHRIST

# Through the Eyes of a Child

Store your treasures in heaven, where moths and rust cannot
destroy, and thieves do not break in and steal. Wherever the
treasure is, there the desires of your heart will also be.
Matthew 6:21–22

Open my eyes to see the wonderful truths in your instruction.
Psalm 119:18

~~~~~

She is two and one half, going on three,
A child who loves exploring her world.
Her bright blue eyes miss nothing of interest;
Proudly, she carries her treasure box.

Pinecones and leaves, dandelions and sticks—
All are treasures in her mind.
But a child's innocence is fast outgrown
As it adapts to worldly tastes and desires.

Material treasure may become the focus—
Money and things that satisfy wants.
Our souls will shrivel; our hearts will shrink
If we lack the truth that completes our lives.

Christ, our Savior, is the one
Whose light reveals spiritual treasure.
In him, the things we once held dear
Are replaced by virtues that survive death.

Our eyes are opened; priorities shift
To storing treasure that will not perish.
Our spirits mature as we find the freedom
To trust in God for all our needs.

# More Than Meets the Eye

Listen, you who are deaf! Look and see, you blind! …
You see and recognize what is right but refuse to act on it.
You hear with your ears, but you don't really listen.
Isaiah 42:18, 20

I want you to show love, not offer sacrifices. I want you
to know me more than I want burnt offerings.
Hosea 6:6

When he comes, he will open the eyes of the [spiritually]
blind and unplug the ears of the [spiritually] deaf.
Isaiah 35:5

~~~~~

Many times, we examine an object, but we only *look* at it.  We have not really *seen* it; we have missed most of its detail, meaning, or significance.

A tree is more than branches, leaves, and a trunk. It lives in a specific environment; its appearance is unique, even within its species; it meets the needs of the many insects, small animals, and other life that it hosts. We have to get close to it, study it, and learn its secrets in order to more fully understand its role in God's creation.

We learn to see by searching out what is within a thing. The passages of the Bible are meaningless if we just skim over the words. They are meant to be questioned:  What is God saying? How does this relate to the world and to me? Do I need to make attitude or life changes? Other questions relative to the type of passage it is will apply. The answers remain hidden from one who looks without observing, seeing, or considering meaning.

Seeing and hearing is addressed in the scriptures, particularly in the prophetic messages. God's people were performing the sacrificial rituals of their faith, but they did not return his devotion; they were not making the total inner commitment to God that he desired.

In addition, many of the prophecies concerning the messiah were misunderstood. The people yearned for a messiah king who would wrest the control of government from those who oppressed them. But the kingdom Jesus proclaimed had nothing to do with politics. It was a kingdom of the spirit, lived out on earth. He would be a suffering redeemer, as foretold in Isaiah 53. He said to his disciples, "Whoever wants to be a leader among you must be your servant ... For even the Son of Man came not to be served but to serve others and to give his life as a ransom for many."[57]

Jesus called his followers to not only serve others, but to live a life of humility, of godly character; to meet the needs of those who were hungry, lonely, or imprisoned; and to worship in spirit and in truth.

Worship in our own day may be a shallow performance. We may recite creeds and prayers without conscious thought because we know the words so well. But seeing and hearing God in a house of worship, in a spiritual sense, can only happen if one worships from the heart, loving God with all one's heart, soul, mind, and strength.[58] God is only honored by the immersion of his worshippers in his love and goodness and majesty.

Even young children can be taught to look beneath what seems to be. It is delightful to teach them to see the wonders of God in nature. When taken on a walk outside, they love finding "treasures" that lie mostly unnoticed. A spider web is exciting as they observe an insect stray onto its sticky silk threads. As the insect struggles to free itself from the web, it becomes more entangled. The spider senses the vibrations and runs out on the non-sticky threads. She quickly immobilizes the insect with a toxin she produces and, faster than one would think possible, wraps the insect in a silken cocoon. The children are observing the specialized ways small animals fit perfectly into their niches, or places, in creation.

Soon, they are finding treasures on their own. They are learning to search for what lies beneath the surface. When they begin to read scripture, it will be a small jump to look for meaning within it.

Jesus calls us to store up treasures in heaven.[59] A child is capable of providing an example to adults of discerning relative values. He is eager to learn and asks many questions that begin with the word "why." When we love and learn with the intensity of a child, our ability to discern deeper meaning and significance in what we see and hear will continue to grow.

# Rooted in Christ

Blessed are those who trust in the Lord and have made the Lord
their hope and confidence. They are like trees planted along a
riverbank, with roots that reach deep into the water. Such trees are
not bothered by the heat or worried by long months of drought.
Their leaves stay green and they never stop producing fruit.
Jeremiah 17:7–8

Now just as you accepted Christ Jesus as your Lord,
you must continue to follow him. Let your roots grow
down into him, and let your lives be built on him.
Colossians 2:6–7

Out of the stump of David's family will grow a shoot—yes, a new
Branch bearing fruit from the old root. And the Spirit of the Lord will
rest on him–the Spirit of wisdom and understanding, the Spirit of
counsel and might, the Spirit of knowledge and the fear of the Lord.
Isaiah 11:1–2

~ ~ ~ ~ ~

An oak is a productive tree. When mature, its branches spread wide,
providing shelter and food for a wide variety of insects, birds, and small
animals. During a long life, its production of fruit, acorns, is prolific.
In death, it becomes a haven for specialized small plants, insects, fungi,
and bacteria. Eventually, the tree has been pulverized and provides
nourishment as fiber and fertilizer in the soil for a new generation of
oaks, other woodland trees, and wildlife.

The tree begins life as a single leaf that emerges from the ground seeking
sunlight, and a tiny root seeking nourishment in the soil. At this point,
it is vulnerable to life-terminating events—being devoured by an insect,
dried up in a drought, or crowded out by a stronger, more established
plant. If it is growing in a favorable spot, it will thrive.

As it grows taller and more mature, storms assail it. But as its branches bow to the storm, the cells in the wood of the branches become stronger and better able to withstand the next storm. It may be scarred by some of its experiences—an insect invasion or a broken branch in a storm. But God built into the oak, as well as into men and women, a very strong instinct for survival. We hunker down, seeking spiritual resources from deep within ourselves. Our spirits, strengthened and encouraged by the indwelling Holy Spirit, can withstand the storms of life in a way similar to the oak.

The reserves of the oak are contained in the root system. If it is strong and deep, nutrients will be moved up into the trunk and remaining branches, producing new growth. In many trees, new green shoots will sprout all around the base, even from a remnant of the trunk. Prophetic scripture in the book of Isaiah uses this ability to describe the continuation of David's royal family line, which had been decimated by events ordained by God to purify his people. A new shoot who would be the salvation of the world, Jesus, would grow out of the remnant of that family.

If we are firmly rooted in Christ, we may bend with the storms, but we will emerge erect. We will be stronger in Christ than before and, more than that, able to spread acorns of faith and comfort by helping others through their storms in the same way the Lord has helped us.[60]

# Clothed for Eternity

Put on your new nature, and be renewed as you learn to know
your Creator and become like him ... Clothe yourselves
with tenderhearted mercy, kindness, humility, gentleness
and patience ... Above all, clothe yourselves with love,
which binds us all together in perfect harmony. And let
the peace that comes from Christ rule in your hearts.
Colossians 3:10, 12, 14–15

Think about what is true, and honorable, and right,
and pure, and lovely, and admirable. Think about
things that are excellent and worthy of praise.
Philippians 4:8

~~~~~

When we receive Christ into our lives, and are given a new nature, we are told to "clothe" ourselves with the figurative clothing of Christ-like characteristics and attitudes. The many possible combinations of personality traits, skills, talents, and gifts that make up you and me are too many to number, guaranteeing that each of us is unique. Each is valued equally by God in his or her contribution to the body of Christ.

As we "put on" the emotional and attitudinal characteristics in our new nature in Christ, our personalities become more Christ like. We cannot see these ethereal qualities as we see outer clothing. But they give life, vibrancy, and genuine character to our whole persons.

The mosaic of the facets, or different aspects, of our selves is "glued" together into something beautiful by love. Paul says, "If I had such faith that I could move mountains, but didn't love others, I would be nothing."[61] He names qualities of love, such as these: patience, kindness; lack of jealousy, boastfulness, pride, or irritability; it never gives up or loses faith; it is always hopeful, and endures through every circumstance.[62]

Love is represented biblically by olive oil, as is the Holy Spirit. Olive oil was used in many ways, including in lamps and as medicine. In the parable of the Good Samaritan, olive oil and wine are used to treat a wounded traveler's wounds.[63] It was also used for anointing, as when the prophet, Samuel, used a flask of olive oil to anoint David, who was then tending sheep, as the next king of Israel.[64]

John 4:24 tells us, "God is Spirit." As believers, we are the temple of God and the Spirit of God lives in us.[65] Because we are to clothe ourselves in love, we can picture the living love of the Holy Spirit as permeating our entire selves in unity with Christ as when he prayed in the garden: "I pray that they will all be one, just as you and I are one ... May they be in us ... May they experience such perfect unity that the world will know that you sent me and that you love them as much as you love me."[66]

In Ephesians 4, Paul describes how all this comes together in the body of Christ. As we are instructed to do Christ's work and build up his church, we will come to such maturity and unity in our faith and knowledge of Jesus that we will be mature in Christ and measure up to his standard. "We will speak the truth in love, and grow in every way more and more like Christ, who is the head of his body, the church. He makes the whole body fit together perfectly. As each part does its own special work, it helps the other parts grow, so that the whole body is healthy and growing and full of love."[67]

# Treasure Box

O Father, Lord of heaven and earth, thank you for hiding
these things from those who think themselves wise and
clever, and for revealing them to the childlike.
Luke 10:21

[God] graciously gave me the privilege of telling the Gentiles
about the endless treasures available to them in Christ.
Ephesians 3:8

Your instructions are more valuable to me
than millions in gold and silver.
Psalm 119:72

~ ~ ~ ~ ~

The box was filled, then set aside.
Its precious collection of trivia
From sunlit field and shaded woods
All became treasures in his box.

Time moved on; the child grew;
Worldly things seized his thoughts.
The simple pleasures of his youth
Were lost in the busyness of daily life.

Years later, the box was found;
Long-lost memories flooded his mind
Of wandering slowly, looking about,
Reveling in beauty in every direction.

He gave the box to his own curious child,
His innocence untouched by the realities of life.
The treasures inside from field and woods
Were as fresh to him as the day they were found.

The majesty of God's creation
Must be enjoyed with thoughtfulness.
Take time to slow your frenzied pace,
To enjoy each moment as it is given.

A sense of contentment, and peace of mind,
Floods our souls with its healing balm.[68]
In daily renewal alone with God,
The freshness of life will return anew.

# Fulfillment

And God will generously provide all you need. Then you will always
have everything you need and plenty left over to share with others.
II Corinthians 9:8

This same God who takes care of me will supply all your needs from
his glorious riches, which have been given to us in Christ Jesus.
Philippians 4:19

~~~~~

When I feel discouraged, he brings hope.

When I feel pain, he gives comfort.

When I feel slighted, he offers acceptance.

When I am angry, he listens and calms.

When I stray, his love prevails.

He will not let me go;
He chose me for his own
Before my life began.

His love enfolds me; my past is cleansed.

His perfect peace calms my turmoil.

His joy overflows from my heart.

He gives me strength through all my trials.

Life is complete as I live in Christ.

# HEALING MOMENTS

# Healing Moments

A spiritual gift is given to each one of us so we can help each
other … The same Spirit gives great faith to [one], and to
someone else the one Spirit gives the gift of healing.
I Corinthians 12:7, 9

Are any of you sick? You should call for the elders of the
church to come and pray over you, anointing you with
oil in the name of the Lord. Such a prayer offered in faith
will heal the sick, and the Lord will make you well.
James 5:14–15

All glory to God, who is able, through his mighty power at work
within us, to accomplish infinitely more than we might ask or think.
Ephesians 3:20

~ ~ ~ ~ ~

Prayer for healing in illness, for recovery following an accident or
surgical procedure, or for other physical or emotional needs did not
end with the death and resurrection of Jesus. Rather, the Holy Spirit
occasionally heals by his power through our prayers in the present time,
in our contemporary, unbelieving world.

Current scientific knowledge does not fully understand all the factors
involved in the body's essentially miraculous self-healing powers. To
call on God for spiritual healing requires genuine faith; healing is a
gift from God, subject to his will. I have seen people heal more quickly
than doctors expected after surgery or an accident many times. I have
also participated in prayer for healing where the results were beyond
anything we could understand with our current knowledge.

Many years ago, I heard about a ten-year-old boy, a friend of the family,
who was hospitalized with a seriously infected eye. He had been playing
in a cornfield with friends, throwing chunks of debris at each other.
Something had worked its way into his eye and was causing him great

pain. He underwent exploratory surgery. He was on massive amounts of antibiotics. But nothing had been successful in locating the source of the infection or alleviating it. The next step, if necessary, was to be the removal of his eye.

In a small circle of women who met regularly for prayer, we lifted him in prayers of healing. His mother later reported that as he lay on his bed, at about the time we prayed, a large piece of cornstalk worked its way out of his eye onto his cheek. He told his mother, "It just fell out, and it didn't even hurt!" His doctor was overjoyed. He was released from the hospital later that day with his eye intact and with perfect vision.

An incident like this is difficult to explain or rationalize. It can only be taken at face value. A young boy was in danger of losing his eye to surgery, and now he could see perfectly with both eyes.

At another time, a friend asked for prayers for her two-week-old baby boy. He had a kidney malfunction that could require surgery. In the next week, he was going to undergo additional tests to determine what might be needed to correct the problem. Two other friends and I stood around her and prayed for healing. The results of the tests the following week were negative, with no surgery required. Today, the baby is a healthy little boy, burning off energy.

Prayer was sufficient for a young mother who was planning a trip to Europe with her husband when she developed TMJ, a locking of her jaw. Her dentist had said it could take six months to return to normal. She could only eat very soft food. Her plans to enjoy European cuisine were in ruins. She talked about hopes and dashed dreams. Before we parted, we prayed for the healing of her jaw. A few days later, she told me that shortly after we prayed, the jaw relaxed. It has never been a problem in the intervening years.

A proper response to the healing power of God in these, and in response to other prayers for healing of all kinds by faith-filled people, might be "God is good." To try to explain them takes away from the great joy experienced by each person, and from the glory of God exhibited in his gracious response to our prayers.

Throughout God's creation and in our wonderfully complex human bodies, there are poorly understood elements. The growth of a baby from conception through birth is a miracle in itself. Untold mysteries wait to be discovered in the interactions of the universe and in our unique Earth; these generate soaring worship from us as we ponder our place in God's plan. We are the only one of God's creatures given a questing mind, a searching spirit, and a need for relationship with our creator to find true fulfillment.

The question of what constitutes a miracle is sometimes ambiguous. On occasion, throughout biblical history, God acted in unusual, spectacular, or even supernatural ways, such as when he provided manna to the Israelite people for a time. Jesus provided loaves and fishes for a hungry crowd and healed many hurting people. But mostly, God works within his natural laws.[69] These encompass the interrelationships of all the elements of sky and sea, plants and animals, and how humankind cares for the world we live in. Often, the effective working together of the elements of God's creation is compromised, producing undesired results.

Studies on faith and healing show that the best healing takes place when a person lives so that a properly aligned soul and spirit can direct bodily healing provided by good medical care. Prayer for the sick and suffering should praise God for the intricate mechanisms of healing that are present in the body. We can then pray that God's special grace will give the whole person the ability to use these resources to his or her best advantage.[70]

Healing takes on forms other than the physical. It embraces acceptance and dependence, emotional grief of many kinds, the forgiveness of sin, and the healing of memories. In all of these, Jesus is the source shining bright; we are seekers of his truth and life. We are instructed to tell God what we need, and thank him for all he has done. Then we will experience God's peace, which exceeds anything we can understand.[71]

That peace itself brings a kind of healing. We no longer struggle for what will not or cannot be. In our acceptance of what is, the Holy Spirit floods our spirit with peaceful joy. We are complete in Christ, even if our prayers are not answered exactly as we conceived them.

Nothing can match the love, care, and protection of our savior and Lord, comforter and counselor, Jesus Christ. We have one life in which to find the joy of the Lord and live the life we are given to the fullest, improving our circumstances as we are guided.

# EPILOGUE

# JESUS

King of kings, Lord of lords,
Name above all names,
Before whom every knee shall bow.

He satisfies my need as fresh water in the heat.

His comfort blankets me when I am in distress.

He fulfills my longings by showering me with love.

He smoothes the troubles, bumps, and bruises
In my life as He stilled the angry sea.

His compassionate love for me is beyond understanding.

His mercy is immeasurable, covering all my sins.

His care is as faithful as the passing of the seasons.

He is sovereign,
Before whom every knee shall bow,
Name above all names,
King of kings and Lord of lords.

# Endnotes

1   J. I. Packer, Merrill C. Tenney, and William White Jr., *The Bible Almanac* (Nashville, TN: Thomas Nelson Publishers, 1980), 397, 407.

2   Acts 17:28.

3   Ephesians 1:19–23.

4   The word, "remains", may also be translated "abides". "It describes a profound, intimate, and enduring relationship … We cannot gain the permanence of our relationship by our own effort; this relationship is only made permanent by the gracious initiative of God indwelling our lives through his Spirit. This means commitment on the part of both God and the disciple. The mutual indwelling between God and the believer is … an enduring, permanent, and eternal relationship." New Living Translation, *NLT Study Bible*, 2nd ed. (Carol Stream, IL: Tyndale House Publishers, 2008), 1803.

5   Psalm 139:16.

6   Joshua 1:5.

7   Luke 22:39–44.

8   Mark 15:34.

9   Mark 15:37–38 "If the curtain was the interior curtain that tore, it was probably a sign that, just as the heavens were split for Jesus to reveal his direct access to God," [at the time of his baptism: Mark 1:10–11] "his death now extended this access to his followers. (Hebrews 6:19, 20)." New Living Translation, *NLT Study Bible*, 1692.

10  Ephesians 1:19–20.

11  Matthew 25:34–40.

12  "Salvation" is defined as deliverance from the power and effects of sin, danger, or difficulty by God's intervention. New Living Translation, *NLT Study Bible*, 2458.

13  Acts 10:34.

14  John 1:12.

15  Jeremiah 29:13.

16  Turning from one's selfish way involves allowing Jesus to determine one's goals and purposes in life. To "take up your cross" is a metaphor that indicates "that faithfulness to Jesus must extend, if required, even to the point of death." Following Jesus's teaching and example is a continuing commitment. New Living Translation, *NLT Study Bible*, 1666.

17  II Corinthians 3:18.

18  Ephesians 3:17.

19  I Peter 5:4.

20  Hebrews 12:12–14.

21    Isaiah 40:31.

22    I John 4:18.

23    Proverbs 15:8.

24    Psalm 40:8.

25    Isaiah 65:24.

26    Matthew 6:8.

27    Acts 4:21–22.

28    Psalm 91:2, 4.

29    Psalm. 23:4–6.

30    Ephesians 2:10.

31    I Thessalonians 5:18.

32    Philippians 4:13.

33    Jeremiah 31:33.

34    Romans 6:13.

35    Luke 19:10.

36    I John 4:10.

37    Ephesians 2:10.

38    John 1:5.

39    Ephesians 6:12.

40    I John 5:4.

41    John 16:33.

42    Matthew 4:1–14 (temptation of Jesus).

43    Ephesians 6:10–18 (armor of God).

44    Jeremiah 29:13.

45    Hebrews 11:1.

46    Psalm 25:9.

47    Ephesians 1:22.

48    New Living Translation, *NLT Study Bible*, 900–905.

49    "Jesus told parables, and those who believed understood while those who had rejected Jesus found that his parables intensified their unbelief ... They lacked the faith that perceives the truth and acts upon it." New Living Translation, *NLT Study Bible*, 1604.

50    Yancy, Philip, *Prayer: Does It Make Any Difference?* (Grand Rapids, Michigan 49530: Zondervan, 2006), 87.

51    Yancy, *Prayer,* 88.

52    John 16:33.

53    Romans 5:3–4.

54    II Timothy 1:6.

55    Proverbs 24:12.

56    Philippians 4:11–12.

57    Matthew 20:26, 28.

58    Matthew 22:37.

59    Matthew 6:19–21.

60    II Corinthians 1:4.

61    I Corinthians 13:2.

62     I Corinthians 13:5–7.

63     Luke 10:34.

64     I Samuel 16:13.

65     I Corinthians 3:16.

66     John 17:21, 23.

67     Ephesians 4:15, 16.

68     The balm of Gilead was an extremely fragrant resinous substance extracted from the balsam tree. It was highly valued among ancient people. The balsam was a bushy evergreen growing twelve to fourteen feet high. The pale yellow gum was used as incense and dissolved in water as an ointment. The oil obtained from the bark, leaves, and berries was used as medicine. This medicinal "balm" is referred to in Jeremiah 8:33 and 51:8 as a symbol of spiritual healing. Packer, Tenney, and White Jr., *Bible Almanac*, 249, 250.

69     Yancy, *Prayer*, 256.

70     Yancy, *Prayer*, 261.

71     Philippians 4:6–7.

Manufactured By:    RR Donnelley
Momence, IL  USA
January, 2011